THE ENCYCLOPEDIA OF
MUSICAL INSTRUMENTS

WOODWIND & BRASS INSTRUMENTS

Produced by Carlton Books Limited

20 Mortimer Street

London, W1N 7RD

Text and Design copyright © Carlton Books Limited 2001

First published in hardback edition in 2001 by Chelsea House Publishers, a subsidiary of
Haights Cross Communications. Printed and bound in Dubai.

First Printing

1 3 5 7 9 8 6 4 2

The Chelsea House World Wide Web address is http://www.chelseahouse.com

Library of Congress Cataloging-in-Publication Data applied for

Woodwind and Brass Instruments ISBN: 0-7910-6091-8

Stringed Instruments ISBN: 0-7910-6092-6

Percussion and Electronic Instruments ISBN: 0-7910-6093-4

Keyboard Instruments and Ensembles ISBN: 0-7910-6094-2

Non-Western and Obsolete Instruments ISBN: 0-7910-6095-0

THE ENCYCLOPEDIA OF
MUSICAL INSTRUMENTS

WOODWIND & BRASS
INSTRUMENTS

ROBERT DEARLING

Chelsea House Publishers

Philadelphia

THE ENCYCLOPEDIA OF
MUSICAL INSTRUMENTS

WOODWIND & BRASS
INSTRUMENTS

Stringed Instruments

Percussion and Electronic Instruments

Keyboard Instruments and Ensembles

Non-Western and Obsolete Instruments

CONTENTS

Introduction:

How Music Began 6

The Making of Instruments 8

Pre-Christian Instruments 10

Instruments and Society 12

Dissemination and Experimentation 14

Woodwind and Brass Instruments 16

Flute 17

Oboe 20

Clarinet 24

Bassoon 28

Saxophone 30

Horn 32

Trumpet 36

Trombone 40

Tuba 42

Rare Brass 44

Index 46

HOW
Music Began

THE EARLIEST MUSIC evaporated into the air, undocumented and unrecorded. Thousands of years of music is thus unknown to us. We cannot even say when it began, for music was in the world centuries before anyone invented writing; that was the Sumerians, in about 3600 BC. Neanderthal man, who disappeared from the Earth some 30,000 years before the Sumerians, may have played with noise-making instruments – it is difficult to imagine him not doing so. But homo sapiens, who replaced Neanderthal man, was superstitious. He had his deities, and would have danced round camp fires and worshipped en masse, probably to instrumental accompaniment. That he had the sensibility to appreciate some art forms is borne out by the figurines (dating from at least 30,000 BC) that have been discovered across Europe, and by the famous cave paintings in south-west France and north-east Spain which appeared by 16,000 BC. Even earlier, a pictorial representation of what might be a musician existed in the caves of Les Trois-Frères.

The first music was undoubtedly vocal. By shouting to one another, men would automatically alter the pitch of their tone to convey different meanings. This would not have been classed as 'music', but when this shouting occurred within the walls of a ravine or against the foot of cliffs, the echo it produced would have intrigued the shouters. They would have repeated their shouts just for the sake of hearing the mysterious answers, and different notes would have been invented for the fun of it. Shouting and chanting during festive dances to celebrate success in the hunt would inevitably have resulted in a predictable rhythm being created by clapping, stamping and slapping parts of the body. Obtuse would have been the man sitting by a log who could have resisted beating out an accompanying rhythm on the log with a stick. In turn, he would have been imitated by the clashing of spears and clubs. He, perhaps, was our first musician; the log, perhaps, our first musical instrument.

These men would have made their music out of everyday objects. Probably by accident, a rock would be hit by a club and produce an unexpected ringing tone which would then be used as a signal to warn of danger. Hollow tree trunks would fulfil the same requirement. In the hunt, men would need to keep account of the whereabouts of the rest of the tribe and would signal their positions by blowing on a conch shell, its sound carrying much further than would a shout. Perhaps a system of rhythmic signals was devised to indicate the location of prey or the direction the hunt was taking – two blasts for 'left', three for 'right', repeated notes for a kill, and so on. Such signals survive today, more reliant upon dif-

THE ANCIENT CONCH SHELL TRUM-PET CONTINUES TO HAVE WIDE CEREMONIAL APPLICATIONS FROM MEXICO TO POLYNESIA.

sion of sounds – the first 'tune' – or grass might be used as a noise-maker when held rigid between the fingers and blown. The next step was to create instruments rather than just stumble across them. It is possible, though unprovable at this distance of time, that the step was taken when an anklet was fashioned from tiny rattles (nut shells, with the dried nuts still inside) to be worn during dance festivals. ♭ᵌ

CAVEMEN CELEBRATING SUCCESS IN THE HUNT. THE HUNTER'S AND WARRIOR'S BOW STRING WOULD RESOUND AS THE ARROW WAS SENT ON ITS WAY.

ferent tones to convey greater subtleties perhaps, but still with origins in prehistory.

Music, if such it can be called, had a useful purpose and possibly even a warlike one, as when conch shells were blown to intimidate an enemy. Man was not always on the move, however. His prime concern, of course, was the desperate need to survive. He had to protect himself and his family from the climate, hunger,

predatory animals and marauding tribes, and what time was left in each day had to go towards improving his comfort. Even so, he found time for art. The figurines mentioned above may have fulfilled a ritual purpose, as the cave paintings probably related to the desire for successful hunting, but some have a grace and delicacy of line that suggest an appreciation of beauty.

In their primitive shelters, sometimes their movement restricted by weather conditions or long winter nights, they would amuse themselves by putting objects to a use for which they were not designed. Stones and rocks within a cave might be hit in a given order to make a succes-

THE EARLIEST
Instruments

%

STONE GONG: a boulder or 'hanging stone' which, when struck, gives off a ringing sound. Oriental and African cultures still use stone as a sound-producer.

TREE STUMP: in certain conditions a hollow tree stump struck with a club would yield a tone.

BRANCHES: the branches of some trees, when flexed and released, will 'twang'. There is a report of a Siberian bear doing this for its own amusement.

GRASS: a blade of grass stretched between fingers or thumbs will emit a high-pitched squeal when blown. This is the origin of the reed principle in woodwind instruments.

CONCH SHELL: often empty when found on a beach, a shell with a broken tip would produce a loud sound when blown. The conch shell trumpet is still found in use today among some primitive peoples.

REEDS: in certain circumstances, reeds and grasses give off a hum when wind blows through them. This is the basis of the Aeolian harp.

BAMBOO: hollow or split bamboo canes will sometimes produce a series of tones in a breeze. The Aeolian organ was thus invented by nature.

THE MAKING OF

Instruments

LONG WINTER NIGHTS spent sitting round a fire in a cave would have been intolerably boring if men had not amused themselves by playing with the objects all about them. Survival may have been of prime interest to them, but with the security of the family and the tribe not in jeopardy there would have been time for experimentation. A cooking pot, gently tapped with a stick, would give off a pleasant sound, and much hilarity would be occasioned as the tone was changed by the addition, then subtraction, of liquid in the pot. Discarded animal skins lay all about. Some would be used as clothing but had to be dried out, a process aided by beating. If the skin was taut it would give a note when beaten. Our experimenting man would have fastened a fragment of skin across the top of the pot and hit it with a stick or drummed on it with his fingers. The first drum had been invented.

A hunting bow string would be plucked to yield a note, and if another string were attached at different points on the bow, a new note was created. The first bow harp had been made. Countless variations suggested themselves to those early experimenters: several strings to the

bow; a pot or gourd attached to the bow to amplify the sound, perhaps a modification accidentally discovered when the end of a bow was stood on a pot; the string struck with a stick to make a string drum; the joining of two bows with a transverse stick at the top, with strings running to the stick, making a lyre, and so on. One particularly sophisticated experiment involved application of a resin, exuded from a tree trunk, applied to a bow string, this string then rubbed crossways on another bow string. The scratchy sound would have needed much experimentation, but eventually a smooth vibrating sound would emerge from this earliest viol.

℅ Music and Magic

After a meal, a straight leg bone might be prepared as a flute. With marrow removed and holes cut at intervals along its length, sounds would emerge when the instrument was blown. This led to the recorder family. Later, one or two reeds were fitted into the recorder's mouthpiece, giving rise to the oboe family, the reeds perhaps being tough grass or slivers of wood found lying on the cave floor. Other experimentation led to the flute, played cross-ways rather than straight out from the mouth.

Gradually, these early musical instruments spread, and with their fame came a certain respect, even fear, for their makers. Magic powers were believed to reside in the instruments, for most members of the tribe, familiar only with thigh-slapping, stamping and log-banging as accompaniments to their dancing rituals, would find the creation of noises from devices they did not understand deeply disturbing. Players of

instruments, too, became mysterious and objects of fear and veneration, and they would not have been human if they had not played on this fear to increase their personal power. Thus, music and magic became inextricably entangled.

Musician-magicians wearing hideous masks and head dresses, would shake gourd rattles, rub serrated wooden sticks together and, most frightening of all because inexplicably it produced a 'sound out of nothing', whirl bull-roarers round their heads to cow 'lower' members of the tribe. Witch-doctors and chiefs became the main disseminators of music, albeit music to be feared rather than enjoyed. All these instruments – gourd rattles, scrapers and bull-roarers – have been found in late Paleolithic deposits (made some 30,000 years ago) in Europe.

Later, voice-disguisers were used to scare the tribe. A wooden trumpet protruding from a mask and acting as a megaphone would give out orders and cast spells, the witch-doctor's voice grotesquely distorted into something regarded as supernatural. Sometimes a friction drum would be used, its harsh grating sound designed yet again to induce fear. But not all 'music' was fearful. The bow, much reduced in size and applied to the mouth, was more of a toy than a serious instrument, and from this came later developments during the Iron Age, such as the Jew's harp. The various early harps were also enjoyed as friendly family entertainment, and probably accompanied long verbal sagas of tribal historical events. ₿

PURPOSE-MADE PRIMITIVE *Instruments*

℅

BONE: an animal or human bone, suitably dried and emptied of marrow, then drilled with finger holes, created the early recorder and flute.

MEMBRANE: any animal skin or tough leaf, when stretched and beaten, will resonate to give out a sound.

POT: a cooking pot struck with a stick will ring out a note which changes as the pot is filled with liquid. If a membrane is stretched across the mouth, the pot is converted into a drum. Pottery drums, with or without membranes, are widely distributed among primitive cultures.

BOW: the hunter's bow normally resounds when an arrow is released. Early experimenters would have altered the tension of the string, shortened its length, and added a resonator. This was the origin of countless different models of lute, harp and lyre. With tree sap rubbed on the string and another bow applied cross-ways, the bow would produce a note. Thus, viol and violin families began.

GOURD: like the cooking-pot, the gourd lends itself to musical deployment. It can be struck, made into a drum, filled with pebbles and shaken, blown like an *ocarina*, or used as a resonator.

MAGIC AND SUPERSTITION WERE DECISIVE FACTORS IN THE DEVELOPMENT OF MUSIC AND IN TRIBAL DISCIPLINE. WITCH DOCTORS IN NEW GUINEA STILL FULFIL THESE FUNCTIONS.

LEFT: A GOURD RATTLE, ITS HUMANOID MASK-LIKE FACE FASHIONED TO MAKE THE TRIBE BELIEVE IT POSSESSES A SOUL OF ITS OWN.

PRE-CHRISTIAN

Instruments

ONCE THE HABIT of making instruments, rather than finding them, became widespread there was an explosion of activity outwards from the centres in the Middle East and Europe. Again, firm dates cannot be established because records were not kept; neither can an exact chronology be suggested. But it is clear that experimentation became the order of the era.

Drummers, once satisfied with a single tone when stick hit log, sought to widen their repertoire. One way was to hollow out a log through a longitudinal slit and leave the two lips of the slit

with different thicknesses of wood and different widths of inner overhang. Each lip would then give a distinct note. By varying the thickness of each lip along the drum's length, several notes could be obtained. Because drums are relatively easy to make, dozens of different types soon emerged, some with membranes, some without. This instrument's shape also varied enormously, noteably that of primitive drums. The recognized names for drum types clearly indicate their shape, for example, the barrel drum and the conical drum.

Adventurous instrument makers would shun the lowly hunter's bow and make a purpose-built stringed instrument with a gourd resonator permanently attached. The spike fiddle is a fairly basic design, in the same way early harps are, but lyres and lutes soon reached improved levels of sophistication as man became aware of the importance of pitch. In singing, uncontrolled ululation had yielded to a vocalization in which rudimentary scales and the satisfying relation of one note to another were realized, so instruments had to play 'in tune' with the singers if they were to be accepted.

Similar rules applied to blown instruments. Random drilling of finger holes in a bone or wooden flute soon proved ineffective. They had to be drilled at certain points and of a certain diameter if the instrument were to be successful. It is possible that an important factor was the

A WALL PAINTING IN THE TOMB OF NEBAMUN, THEBES, SHOWING MUSICIANS WITH LUTES, 1400 BC.

OLD-WORLD (c.3000BC) Instruments

BLOW: bone and wooden flutes (side-blown and end-blown), gourd flute (ancestor of the *ocarina*), recorder (end-blown), whistle, bird lure, panpipes, single- and double-reed pipes (ancestors of the clarinet and oboe families); animal-horn trumpet and horn, from about 20cm (8 inches) to the length of an elephant tusk; metal trumpet.

PLUCK: harp, lute, lyre; bamboo *zither* (formed by separating outer fibres and inserting bridges); mouth harp (many varieties, leading to the Jew's harp); string drum (might also be beaten); thumb piano (springy metal tongues in a resonator).

SCRAPE: friction drum (a pulled cord running from a membrane); wooden scraper with serrated edge; rattle (with wood or metal tongues flexed against a rotating cog); ?fiddle.

BANG: drums, with or without membranes; xylophone (wooden slats over a frame or pit); stamping tube (bamboo, or similar, bounced endways); ground 'harp' (wooden boards over a pit, struck with beaters or dancing feet; also beaten cords across a pit); mouth bow (a short bow, held endways in the mouth and struck with a stick); bells (wood, metal, with clapper or struck with beater); *maracas* (small wooden dish-shaped objects clashed together).

WHIRL: bull-roarer

SHAKE: rattles (open, with loose objects striking a frame or shaken freely; or closed, with hard objects inside a gourd, drum, pot, etc.); *sistrum* (early Egyptian 'Y'-shaped frame with captive metal or wood discs on wires).

need to imitate bird song correctly, for if a bird lure did not faithfully mimic the song of its intended victim it would fail. And it was all well and good to blow loud rasps through an animal horn, but by shaping the mouthpiece in a certain way to accommodate the lips effectively, more controlled sounds would result.

By 3000 BC at the latest instrument making had evolved from being a pastime into a disciplined craft. Soon it would be an art.

Having established a wide range of instruments it is only natural that man would wish to combine their sounds in some kind of group. Most obvious would have been a 'melody instrument' of some kind, probably a pipe, with a rhythmic accompaniment. As in much jazz, the lead would have been taken by the 'rhythm section' (a man hitting a log) and the piper would have adopted his rhythm. Simple enough, but each would have had to listen to the other.

Add more instruments and confusion threatened. Some control became vital. A leader would be elected, or elect himself, to direct the performance. He would have dictated rhythm and tempo (modern concepts yet to be fully comprehended) and suppressed an instrumentalist if he considered his playing too loud or otherwise unsatisfactory. How he did this is not clear, but stamping, arm waving, facial signals and threats were doubtless involved. Thus, these early leaders created order out of potential chaos, as do conductors today.

Concrete evidence of instruments of c.3000 BC comes from Sumerian drawings and remains. The Sumerians had bow harps, lyres, drums and clappers, and possibly flutes. Sophisticated lutes came later. Egypt knew the flute by that date and, shortly afterwards, *aulos*, harp, lyre, *sistrum* and other percussion. Tutankhamun's trumpets (one bronze, the other silver) date from c.1300 BC.

A LYRE PLAYER DEPICTED ON THE STANDARD OF UR (SUMERIA), c. 2600 BC: IN FRONT A ROYAL OFFICIAL, BEHIND A FEMALE SINGER.

Instruments AND Society

ACCORDING TO THE BIBLE (Daniel 3: 5, 7, 10, 15), Nebuchadnezzar owned an orchestra in Babylon in the 6th century BC. It consisted of "horn, pipe, lyre, trigon, harp, bagpipe, and every kind of music". The details of this ensemble, written down in Aramaic four centuries later and then translated into obsolete English, cannot be taken literally. However, this reference does illustrate two important points. First, the 18th-century custom of noble and royal courts supporting an orchestra has an ancient precedent; secondly, the existence of an orchestra so long ago was remarkable enough to be noted and the note handed down to a much later scribe.

Musicologist Curt Sachs gave a new interpretation of this Aramaic text in *The History of Musical Instruments* (1942). He suggested that, rather than enumerating the composition of an orchestra, the text gave a description of a performance: "a horn signal, followed by solos of oboe, lyre and harp, and a full ensemble of these and some rhythmical instruments." – see panel.

The Greek theorist Aristoxenus (fl 375–360 BC), working on Pythagoras's tuning system of two centuries earlier, helped to establish tuning principles. These encouraged makers to build better instruments. The bards, poets and singers found throughout Europe from before Christ were among the chief beneficiaries. Their favoured instrument, the lyre, was made versatile and melodic as a consequence of these sophisticated 'tuning systems', which enabled the instrument to be played at the same time as a spoken or sung narration.

In the Christian era advances in instrumental design continued to be made, and the use of instruments became more widespread. People became accustomed to them as part of their daily lives, for both pleasure and utilitarian purposes. Pipers, lute players and fiddlers would frequent taverns and inns in the hope of receiving a copper or two 'to wet the whistle' (though pedants may aver that 'whistle' in this context was Saxon *hwistle*, from Latin *fistula* = 'windpipe', the Latin word also means pipe in the wider, musical, sense). Pipers would busk in the streets for the same purpose.

A 14TH-CENTURY DEPICTION OF A HYDRAULIS OR WATER ORGAN; SEE PAGE 230 FOR FURTHER DETAILS.

A civic vacuum was created by the departure of the Romans from their European colonies during the fifth century. The realization that security was needed for their towns moved local committees of elders to set up a system of criers. The task of these men would be to warn of fire, flood or attack. Equipped with bells, horns and whistles they would patrol town streets at night, marking the time with the bell and sounding their wind instruments in the event of an impending threat. The use of sounds to warn of danger has been with us since time immemorial. Bells had been used by lepers to warn others of their approach. In our own century whistles have been used to raise the alarm or warn of attack, and church bells would have been rung in the event of a German invasion of Britain during World War II. In earlier centuries, posthorns sounded a happier arrival, that of the mail coach.

As civilization developed in post-Roman Europe, instruments accompanied civic occasions such as parades and proclamations. Street vendors would advertise their wares with shouts and also sometimes with instruments: in a busy market place the loudest noise secures the greatest attention. Military camps possibly used instrumental calls at reveille; this became a regular procedure after the return from the Crusades of soldiers who had encountered such practices in the Middle East. Marching to the sound of a drum to keep in step had been learnt from the Romans, however. Trumpets would announce officers' orders during battle; trumpets and drums remain the mainstay of military bands.

Some religions and cults forbade instrumental music in church, considering the playing of instruments a frivolous activity unsuited to sacred buildings. Others embraced it as a welcome enrichment to the singing of chants; sometimes also as contrast in the interludes between hymns and sermons. The deep, sonorous voice of the sackbut was particularly effective. The organ, too, still hand-pumped, was an almost inevitable fixture: it gave an even greater feeling of solemn splendour as well as reminding the choir of the opening phrase of the next hymn.

Domestic music-making was more common in the 8th century than it is today, for there were fewer distractions. Cheap or home-made stringed instruments, drums and pipes were found in the majority of homes. In the open air, pagan fertility festivals were danced to instrumental accompaniment, and at wild boar and wolf hunts the sound of primitive horns and trumpets would have been heard.

Nebuchadnezzar's Orchestra

6TH CENTURY BC

𝄋

ORIGINAL NAME (PHONETIC)	ACCEPTED TRANSLATION (RV)	CURT SACHS' INTERPRETATION
quarna	horn	horn or trumpet (cf Latin *cornu*= horn
masroquita	pipe	pipe (from verb *sriquá*=to whistle; cf Middle English *scritch*= screech, shriek
qatros	lyre	lyre (cf Greek *kithara*)
sabka	trigon	horizontal angle harp. The word *sabka* also meant a naval war machine, a boat with a vertical ladder at one end. The instrument's tuning pegs would have suggested ladder rungs, and strings stretching from 'mast' to 'deck' would have completed the triangle suggested in *trigon*.
psantrin	harp	vertical angle harp (cf Greek *psalterion*).
sumponiah	bagpipe	a 'sounding together' (Greek *symphonia*). The word *symphonia* meaning bagpipe, arose much later, and the same word meaning hurdy-gurdy comes from 12th-century France.
zmara	every kind of music	ensemble, plus rhythm and percussion music.

A TEUTONIC WARRIOR WITH A *LUR* (WAR TRUMPET); FROM THE SARCOPHAGUS OF EMPEROR HOSTILIANUS, DIED 251 AD.

DISSEMINATION AND

Experimentation

BY THE 11TH CENTURY instrumental developments in China, India and probably the yet to be explored continent of Africa, were more varied than those in the West. The Americas were limited to wind and percussion until the Iberians introduced the guitar family there. Europe was emerging from the Dark Ages and experiencing a flowering of vocal music. In France, Germany, England and northern Italy from around 1100, the Goliards travelled from town to town, court to court, singing to their own accompaniment on harps and veilles, transportable instruments of light tone against which they sang their poems of secular delights. Carl Orff raided these poems, which he dressed in his own brilliant orchestral colours, for his *Carmina Burana* (1937).

In southern France from c.1100 to c.1300 the troubadours (from *trouver*, to find or invent, because they travelled the land finding folk tales and melodies and inventing their own brands of both) also played such instruments, plus pipes, hurdy-gurdys and drums. The *trouvères* (from c.1137 to c.1400) were, like the troubadours, high-born and well-educated – some, indeed, were reigning princes. They ranged more widely over France and other areas of north-west Europe.

German poets also took up the life of wandering minstrels, singing to their own accompaniment. The Minnesingers (from c.1180 to c.1500), and the Mastersingers (from 1311 to the 17th century), all spread jollity with their bawdy and witty songs, carrying with them every portable instrument available. At the courts they would have met up with resident musicians who would have joined in the merry-making. Many of the poems survive; rather fewer of the melodies. No instrumental directions were written down, so we have to rely upon clues as to what music accompanied the voices. A great deal may be gleaned from the types of instruments available in those days, and modern revivers of such music would do well to study these and include as many of them as possible. The medieval spirit was predominantly robust and it is a fair assumption that instruments would have been played with more enthusiasm than subtlety.

Although purveying primarily a vocal art,

MINNESINGERS AT THE WARTBURG SINGING CONTEST C. 1206. PRESENT WERE HEINRICH VON OFTERDINGEN, WOLFRAM VON ESCHENBACH AND WALTER VON DER VOGELWEIDE.

BERNARD DE VENTADORN, POSSIBLY THE FINEST TROUBADOUR. HE SERVED ELEANOR OF AQUITAINE, WIFE OF HENRY PLANTAGENET, AND BECAME A MONK LATE IN LIFE.

these itinerant poets were vitally important in the dissemination and popularization of instruments. By introducing them to outlying areas as well as palaces, they familiarized countless communities with their qualities and encouraged others to play and to make instruments. They also brought about far-reaching improvements in instrumental construction and design. The hard life of travelling on rough tracks would have made these poets find ways of strengthening delicate lutes; varying weather conditions would have suggested better and quicker ways of tuning; and the different moods and circumstances found at successive courts would have demanded versatility, resulting in cross-fertilization of playing techniques between different types of instrument.

With our instrumental history poised at the threshold of further important developments we may take stock. Lute, lyre, hurdy-gurdy, fife, cornett and many others were becoming obsolete. The violin family was set to displace the viols, and great improvements in wind instruments were soon to appear. The modern orchestra was being conceived. 𝄢

TRAVELLING POETS OF THE *Middle Ages*

GOLIARDS, c.1100–c.1250
HUGH PRIMAS (c.1095–1160+), whose reported deformed features may account for the mordant nature of his poems.
SERLO OF WILTON (c.1110–c.1181), an Englishman teaching in Paris who became so sickened with his own erotic poems that he became a monk.
ARCHIPOETA (c.1130–1165+), a pseudonym of a punning *goliard* from Cologne.

TROUBADOURS, c.1100–c.1300
DUKE GUILHEM IX OF AQUITAINE (1071–1127), who "was much addicted to jesting, and surpassed the innumerable pranks of the greatest clowns. He knew well how to sing and make verses and ... deceive the ladies."
BERNART DE VENTADORN (1125–1195), probably the finest poet of the troubadours. Some of his poems were adopted by Minnesingers.
GUIRAUT DE BORNEIL(L) (c.1140–c.1200), called *maistre dels trobadors*.
COUNT RAIMBAUT III OF ORANGE (c.1144–1173), consort of Countess Beatriz.
COUNTESS BEATRIZ OF DIA (late 12th century), the only woman troubadour to have a complete song preserved.
GUIRAUT RIQUIER (c.1230–c.1294), a morose character whose playing and singing gave a deceptively joyful impression.

TROUVERES, c.1137–c.1400
BLONDEL DE NESLE (c.1155/60–?), from northern France, whose melodies show the influence of Gregorian chant.
COLIN MUSET (fl. 1200–1250), a *jongleur*, or juggler, whose manual dexterity doubtless extended to the playing of instruments.
ADAM DE LA HALE (c.1250–c.1288?), 'The Hunchback of Arras', composer of the dramatic pastoral *Le jeu de Robin et Marion*.

Despite this, and the similarity of name, there is no evidence to link him with Alan a'Dale, minstrel of the Robin Hood stories first noted in c.1377.

MINNESINGERS, c.1180–c.1500+
DER VON KÜRENBERG (c.1160–?), an Austrian nobleman.
WALTER VON DER VOGELWEIDE (c1170–c1230), regarded as the most outstanding and influential of the Minnesingers.
GOTTFRIED VON STRASSBURG (fl. 1200–1210), whose epics *Tristan* and *Parzifal* provided Wagner with operatic subjects.
DER TANNHÄUSER (c.1200–c.1270), whose songs tell of his (probably imaginary) exploits as a soldier and crusader. Wagner borrowed him, too.
HEINRICH VON MEISSEN (1250–1318), a clever and virtuosic artist who is regarded by some as the first Mastersinger.

MASTERSINGERS, 1311–17th century
HEINRICH VON MÜGELN (died c.1369+), a poet active in Prague, Buda (Hungary) and Vienna.
HANS FOLZ (c.1435–1513), a barber and surgeon whose poetry was admired by Hans Sachs.
HANS SACHS (1494–1578), a shoemaker who composed over 6000 poems. Richard Wagner immortalized him in the opera *Die Meistersinger von Nürnberg*.

A MEDIEVAL DEPICTION OF A POET-MINSTREL. MORE POEMS THAN MELODIES COMPOSED BY THESE WANDERING ARTISTS SURVIVE.

Woodwind and Brass Instruments

THE WOODWIND AND brass are among the oldest families of instruments in the history of music, probably because of the very simple principle on which they work. In a nutshell, the player blows through a hole in the end of a tube to make the column of air inside vibrate. The actual or effective length of that vibrating column determines the pitch of the sound produced. The name 'woodwind' applies, not surprisingly, to those instruments originally and mostly still made of wood (the flute and saxophone are the obvious exceptions). Similarly, brass instruments were originally made of that material, though these days they are often made of other metals. The other principal difference between the two groups is the means used to set the column of air vibrating. In all woodwind instruments (again, except the flute) a vibrating reed is used, whereas brass players press their lips against a funnel-shaped mouthpiece and blow something akin to a raspberry down it. The usual orchestral woodwind grouping consists of flutes, oboes, clarinets and bassoons, often joined by a piccolo, cor anglais, bass clarinet and contrabassoon, and occasionally a saxophone. A typical brass section consists of French horns, trumpets, tenor and bass trombones and a tuba.

WIND INSTRUMENTS WERE AMONG THE FIRST TO BE GROUPED TOGETHER TO FORM ENSEMBLES. THIS 17TH-CENTURY PROCESSIONAL GROUP INCLUDES FORERUNNERS OF THE BASSOON, OBOE, CLARINET, TRUMPET AND TROMBONE.

FLUTE

THE EARLIEST FLUTE capable of playing a melody of more than two or three notes was discovered recently in a Slovenian cave and dates no less than 45,000 years ago. It was fashioned by a Neanderthal man from the leg bone of a young bear. Although damaged, its four finger-holes show that it was made deliberately for the purpose of making music. The musicologist Curt Sachs claimed that a 9th-century Chinese instrument called the *chi'ih* was actually the oldest transverse flute in history, and there are early depictions from the 2nd and 3rd centuries AD showing 'side-blown' instruments. But this evidence is not conclusive, and not until the 1100s was the instrument regularly illustrated in works of art.

The earliest Western European representations come from Germany, giving rise to the popular term 'German flute'. From here use of the instrument spread throughout Europe. Its common use in England is demonstrated by Henry VIII's famous inventory of instruments. In France the flute was held in very high regard. However, the flute's place among the world's most popular and accesible instruments

was not assured until the 18th century. This stabilizing of the instrument's fortunes was due to the work of the composer and flautist Johann Joachim Quantz, his pupil Frederick the Great of Prussia, himself a distinguished flautist, and later the efforts of instrument-maker Theobald Boehm.

𝄋 Construction

The modern orchestral flute is made in three sections with some sixteen padded keys. Some players still prefer wooden instruments, but it is more common to see metal flutes, usually of silver or a metal alloy, but sometimes of gold and

ORIGINALLY MADE OF WOOD, THE FLUTE IS MORE FAMILIAR AS A METAL INSTRUMENT TODAY.

TYPES OF Flute
𝄋

PICCOLO Half the size of the standard flute, and pitched one octave higher (though it is a transposing instrument, its music being written an octave lower than it sounds). It is fingered the same as the concert flute, with almost the same compass, though its lowest note is usually d". The piccolo came into orchestral use about 1800. Beethoven, in his Fifth Symphony, was one of the first composer's to use it.

TREBLE FLUTE IN G Pitched a 5th above the concert flute, this fills the gap between that and the piccolo. It was introduced in about 1950 to replace the obsolete band flute in B flat.

CONCERT FLUTE IN C The standard modern orchestral flute.

ALTO FLUTE IN G Simply a larger version of the concert flute (but pitched a 4th lower, in G), and with a compass from g to c'''. It has sometimes also been called the 'bass' flute, and has been used in music by Stravinsky (*The Rite of Spring*) and Ravel (*Daphnis and Chloe*).

BASS FLUTE Pitched in C, sounding an octave lower than the concert flute. It is characterized by a double-U head joint, and is held like an ordinary flute but often with a support that allows the player to carry most of the instrument's weight on the right leg.

JACQUES HOTTETERRE, SON OF JEAN, WAS A FLAUTIST AT THE COURT OF LOUIS XIV AND LOUIS XV OF FRANCE.

IN ITS TRANSITION FROM A SIMPLE WOODEN INSTRUMENT, THE TRANS-VERSE FLUTE SOON ACQUIRED SOME QUITE COMPLEX KEYWORK.

occasionally even platinum. Though the form of the modern flute is developed from Boehm's design of around 1847, the instrument as we know it had its beginnings before 1500 when it was a simple cylindrical tube with six finger-holes and a blow-hole or 'embouchure'. The three members of the flute family from this time (bass, alto or tenor and descant sizes have been identifed) had wider bores than the narrow con-temporary fifes, giving a mellow tone well suited to consort music. By about 1650 the skilled hands of the celebrated French instrument maker Jean Hotteterre had begun to trans--form the flute. Intonation had always been a problem, to the extent that com-posers such as Martin Agricola recommended buying sets of instru-ments together to avoid too many discrepancies in tuning. Hotteterre's conically-bored instruments began to address that problem with the first real measure of success. His flutes were constructed in three sec-tions, allowing small adjustments to the length to be made where the sections met. During the 18th cen-

tury experimentation continued with instruments in four sections, three-joint examples with a tun-ing slide, and new finger-holes and keywork, so that by 1800 there was an abundance of differ-ent models of flute available.

✄ *The Boehm Flute*

In 1831 the German goldsmith, jeweller and flautist Theobald Boehm was visiting London where he heard the playing of one Charles

Nicholson junior. The design of Nicholson's flute, a father and son collaboration, featured larger finger-holes than Boehm had seen before, affording a stronger and more stable sound. Recognizing the advantages of the design, Boehm began work straight away and by 1843 his new flute, complete with a largely cylindrical bore and more elaborate keywork, was in pro-duction in Paris and London. The definitive Boehm flute appeared in 1847. Its larger finger-holes were placed according to best acoustical principles and did not sit comfortably under the player's fingers, so Boehm developed a new sys-tem of keys and levers to aid performance. Many players were deterred by the fact that this mecha-nism demanded a new system of fingering, and some tried to develop their own flutes based on earlier instruments. However, it is the Boehm flute that enjoys almost universal favour today.

✄ *In Performance*

It was not until the late 17th and early 18th centuries that composers began to respond seriously to the flute's popularity, though some early music does exist, including two sets of

THEOBALD BOEHM. THE FLUTE HE PRODUCED IN 1847 INCOR-PORATED PRINCIPLES THAT HAVE CONTINUED TO INFLUENCE DESIGN TO THIS DAY.

chansons issued by the French publisher Pierre Attaignant in 1533. The tendency of composers before 1600 not to write with specific instruments in mind and the overwhelming popularity of stringed instruments, especially the violin, during the rise of the Baroque style in the 17th century, meant that it was not until Lully first called for the transverse flute in his ballet *The Triumph of Love* in 1681 that the instrument began to find favour. Bach and Handel frequently used the flute as an *obbligato* instrument, but the first published music of any sort for solo flute was Michel de la Barre's collection of 1702, predictably titled *Pieces for Transverse Flute with Basso Continuo*. Spurred on by the sudden vogue for the flute, several virtuoso players began to make a name for themselves. These included Johann Christoph Denner (also an instrument maker who laid the foundations for the clarinet), Quantz and Mozart's favourite flautist Johann Wendling, the principal player in the Mannheim Court Orchestra during the 1770s.

During the 19th century the flute fell out of fashion. Beethoven and Schubert contributed minor works, including the Serenade, Op. 25 (1801), and the Introduction and Variations, D802 (1824), respectively, but otherwise the flute repertory consisted of lightweight salon or chamber music. It was the French who came to the flute's rescue around the turn of the 20th century when composers like Debussy and Ravel moved away from the grand late Romantic style in favour of more delicate tonal colourings. Debussy included an important flute melody in his orchestral *Prélude à l'après-midi d'un faune* (1892–4) and in 1912 wrote his famous *Syrinx* for solo flute. Many 20th-century composers have since written for the flute, including Luciano Berio, John Cage and Pierre Boulez who have written for some of the century's many virtuoso performers. Among them, of course, is the man almost universally credited with the flute's popularity today, the Irish virtuoso James Galway. 𝄢

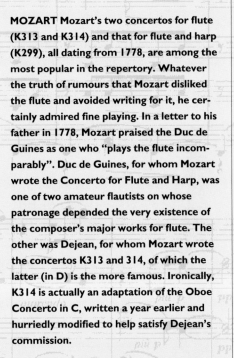

Flute Concertos

VIVALDI Antonio Vivaldi played a seminal part in the development of the concerto, establishing both the prominence of the solo part and a standard three-movement construction. He composed about eighteen flute concertos, though the true designation of some of them has caused debate, for his early publishers tended not to discriminate between those written for flute and those for recorder. Two of the most popular of the eighteen number among those works to which Vivaldi gave a descriptive title: *Il Gardellino* ('The Goldfinch') in D, RV428, and *La tempesta di mare* ('The Stormy Sea') in F, RV433. Both are, in fact, arrangements of earlier works and were probably performed at the Venetian orphanage for girls where Vivaldi worked for much of his career.

QUANTZ The contribution of Quantz to the flute repertory is made remarkable by the sheer volume of his output. Of over 300 concertos, some 277 are known to have been written for Quantz's most celebrated employer and pupil, Frederick the Great. The concertos commonly adhere to the standard three-movement fast-slow-fast form established by Vivaldi and were performed by Frederick, in strict numerical order, at daily court concerts conducted by the composer. Particularly noteworthy are Quantz's delightful long-breathed slow melodies, in which Frederick took special pleasure.

MOZART Mozart's two concertos for flute (K313 and K314) and that for flute and harp (K299), all dating from 1778, are among the most popular in the repertory. Whatever the truth of rumours that Mozart disliked the flute and avoided writing for it, he certainly admired fine playing. In a letter to his father in 1778, Mozart praised the Duc de Guines as one who "plays the flute incomparably". Duc de Guines, for whom Mozart wrote the Concerto for Flute and Harp, was one of two amateur flautists on whose patronage depended the very existence of the composer's major works for flute. The other was Dejean, for whom Mozart wrote the concertos K313 and 314, of which the latter (in D) is the more famous. Ironically, K314 is actually an adaptation of the Oboe Concerto in C, written a year earlier and hurriedly modified to help satisfy Dejean's commission.

IBERT Of the more recent concertos for flute, that by Jacques Ibert is often counted among the masterpieces. Dedicated to the French flautist Marcel Moyse, the work draws on the flute's most expressive qualities. It is an elegant and gracious but impassioned piece that has found a central place in today's repertory. In fact, so quickly was the concerto's value recognized that the third movement was adopted as one of the Paris Conservatoire's infamous *pièces de concours* in 1934, the same year that it was written.

♪ OBOE

WHILE THE FLUTE and its predecessors are known to number among the world's oldest instruments, a pair of Ancient Greek silver pipes, or *auloi*, dating from around the time of 2800 BC, lend reed instruments respectable antiquity. The label 'reed instrument' seems only to have been coined during the Middle Ages, when conical wind instruments using a reed were given the Latin name *calamellus* from *calamus* ('a reed'). Later came the 'shawm' and eventually the French *hoboy* from *hautbois* ('high-', 'strong-' or 'loud-wood'). But the changes in name belie the fact that these were all in essence the same instrument, that which later formed the foundation of the orchestral woodwind section – the oboe. In fact, such were the geographical variations in the use of the instrument's name in the early to mid-1600s that *hautbois* variously described the smaller members of the shawm family as well as the newer instrument, even though the two existed alongside one another for some time, each with a distinct musical purpose.

It is Jean Hotteterre who is commonly credited with the invention, in the mid-1600s, of the oboe proper. Previously the player had little control over the tone of the sound produced, its harsh and rather strident quality making it ideal for outdoor ceremonies and pageants. With the refinements made by Hotteterre and others in France, the sound lost much of its coarseness, and during the 18th century the oboe gradually became fully accepted into the developing mixed ensembles for indoor performances. Into the 19th century the oboe's development became divided between makers in Germany and France, though it was in the latter of these two countries that it underwent its most radical modifications, with makers taking advantage of the rods, axles and key-rings invented by Theobald Boehm.

❀ Construction

Although a number of different models of oboe exist today, the overriding influence of the French makers remains in evidence. Constructed in three sections or 'joints' from grenadilla, rose or cocus wood, the modern oboe has the same narrow bore opening out into a slight bell at the end. It is the highest-pitched member of the double-reed family, which includes the bassoon and which is distinguished from the clarinets and saxophones by, as the name suggests, a double rather than single reed which is held in the player's mouth. Aside from slightly varying characteristics in the bodies of individual oboes, it is the reed which plays the most crucial part in determining the instrument's sound quality or *timbre*. The reed consists of a thin piece of split cane which is folded and shaped and tightly bound to a small tube or 'staple', then inserted into the top of the instrument. While the reed allows the player a great deal of control over the sound produced, that control is one of the most difficult things to master when learning to play the oboe. The reed has only the tiniest of openings at its tip, through which must be forced air at considerable pressure. Oboe players quickly develop strong stomach and cheek muscles!

In medieval instruments the reed and staple were completely enclosed within a shaped wooden block known as a pirouette. This disappeared with Jean Hotteterre's attempts to civilize the shawm during the 1650s, at which time also the instrument's bore became considerably narrower and a thumb-hole was added to the existing six finger-holes. As with the early flutes, players of the first oboes had great difficulty controlling intonation. Perhaps not surprisingly, some of the techniques for improving intonation that were tried for the flute also found their way onto the oboe, notably the supply of upper joints in different lengths, known as *corps de réchange*. Towards the end of the 18th century keywork was designed and added to the oboe by makers such as Jakob Grundmann and Carl Grenser of Dresden. In the first twenty years of the 19th century the number of keys increased to eight, providing alternative fingerings and further improvements in intonation. Then around 1825 the instruments designed by the Viennese player Josef Sellner marked a turning point by increasing the number of keys to thirteen. Sellner's oboe formed the basis of the instrument used throughout Germany during the 19th century, where it continued with very little modification.

♪ THE MODERN OBOE FEATURES ONE OF THE MOST COMPLEX SYSTEMS OF KEYWORK OF ANY WOODWIND INSTRUMENT.

♪ ONE OF THIS CENTURY'S MOST CELE-BRATED OBOISTS, LEON GOOSSENS (PICTURED HERE WITH HIS SISTERS SIDONIE AND MARIE) SHOWS OFF HIS PROWESS WITH AN OBOE IN HIS RIGHT HAND AND A COR ANGLAIS IN HIS LEFT.

TYPES OF
Oboe
§

TREBLE OR SOPRANO OBOE The principal member of the family, pitched in C with a compass of three octaves from *b flat to a'''*.

OBOE D'AMORE Pitched in A, this is the alto member of the family. It originated in Germany, and is known to have been in existence by 1719. Bach used it in some 60 works, beginning with the *St John Passion*. It was obsolete for over 100 years from about 1770, until it was revived in a modern form by Charles Mahillon for 'authentic' Bach performances. The type has found occasional use in 20th-century scores, including Richard Strauss's *Sinfonia domestica*, Debussy's *Images* and Ravel's *Boléro*. John McCabe wrote a Concerto for Oboe d'amore in 1972.

COR ANGLAIS ('ENGLISH HORN') Invented in 1760 by Ferlandis of Bergamo, this is neither English nor a horn but the tenor member of the oboe family. It is a transposing instrument pitched in F, with a compass of about two and a half octaves from e. Not much used before the Romantic period, a number of well-known solos have been written for it since, including Sibelius's *The Swan of Tuonela* and the slow movement of Dvořák's *New World* Symphony.

BARITONE OBOE Originated possibly in the 17th or early 18th century, this is pitched in C, sounding an octave below the soprano oboe. Today its place is often taken by the German heckelphone for use in scores by Richard Strauss (*Elektra* and *Salome*) and Delius (including *Fennimore and Gerda* and *Songs of Sunset*).

✣ The Modern Oboe

In France, meanwhile, at the hands of the craftsmen Henri Brod and Guillaume Triébert the oboe was undergoing fundamental change. Every part of the instrument was redesigned in a succession of different systems, the work of Triébert and his two sons being continued by their company foreman, François Lorée. Despite the attempts of Louis-Auguste Buffet to develop an oboe based on Boehm's revolutionary modifications to the flute, including an enlarged bore and key-holes, it is Lorée's work in developing the 'Conservatoire' model that has remained the key influence in the modern oboe. François' work was continued by his son, Adolphe, in the 20th century.

XXXIX *Ciufolo del Villano*

✣ In Performance

After the early instrument's exclusive use for outdoor performances, the shawm, with its rougher tone, continued in this role, playing folk music in particular. The oboe, however, quickly found its way into the recently developed genre of opera, first appearing in Cambert's *Pomone* in 1671 (though it is sometimes claimed that Lully's ballet *L'amour malade* of 1657 marked its first appearance). It seems to have made its first public appearance in England in a masque called *Calisto* by John Crowne and Nicholas Staggins in 1675, and its first inclusion in a score by Henry Purcell was in the ode *Swifter Isis, swifter flow* in 1681. Purcell's use of the instrument until his death in 1695 is often held up as an example unmatched by his contemporaries. The composer included oboes in all his larger works and wrote at least three major *obbligato* solos for oboe, including a particularly lyrical example in his large-scale ode for the birthday of Queen Mary in 1694, *Come ye sons of art.*

Over the course of the 18th century, as the oboe gradually came to be accepted into the mixed orchestra, its role moved from simply doubling string parts to establishing an expressive and individual solo voice of its own. That very individuality has since

𝄞 EARLY KEYWORK, AS ON THIS THREE-KEYED OBOE, OFTEN ALLOWED FOR FINGERINGS USING 'FISHTAIL' KEYS.

𝄞 THE CHARACTERISTIC STRIDENCY OF THE SHAWM MADE IT PARTICULARLY WELL SUITED TO OUTDOOR PERFORMANCE AND PAGAENTRY.

HENRY PURCELL'S REGULAR USE OF THE OBOE OVER THE LAST 15 YEARS OF HIS LIFE MADE HIM AN UNRIVALLED CHAMPION OF THE INSTRUMENT.

attracted many composers to write fine solo works for the oboe, exploiting both its melancholy and lyrical qualities and its sprightly agility. There are sonatas and concertos by Handel, Vivaldi, Telemann, Giuseppe Sammartini and Bach. Later Mozart wrote his famous Concerto K314 and, probably the highlight of the Classical oboe repertory, the Quartet K370 for oboe and strings (1781) which was exceptional at the time for demanding a top *f‴* from the soloist. Today the oboist's solo repertory is extensive, including well-loved concertos by Richard Strauss, Vaughan Williams and Martinů, and works for unaccompanied oboe, such as Britten's *Six Metamorphoses after Ovid* (1951) and Berio's *Sequenza VII*, an avant-garde *tour de force* from 1969 which demands an extensive range of advanced technical skills.

THE OBOE'S USES IN The Orchestra

The oboe's bright, penetrating sound lends itself to successful characterization in the middle of an orchestral score. Composers have exploited its timbre for everything from evoking pastoral serenity to sheer sound effect.

BEETHOVEN: SYMPHONY NO. 6

On the first page of his manuscript for the Sixth Symphony, Beethoven noted down some observations about programmatic music (music that paints a picture): "The listener should be able to discover the situations for himself", he said, adding the cautionary note, "every kind of painting loses by being carried too far in instrumental music." Nonetheless, the 'Pastoral' Symphony, each of whose five movements bears a descriptive title, is quite explicit in transferring its pictures to music. The second movement Andante, headed 'Scene by the brook', ends with a coda which includes bird calls notated in the score as a nightingale, a quail and a cuckoo, with the part of the quail being taken very effectively by the oboe. This is followed in the third movement, 'A merry gathering of country folk', by a jaunty pastoral theme for solo oboe, accompanied by bassoon and violins, in a passage that clearly sets the scene for the peasants' merrymaking. Incidentally, Beethoven's quail is not the first use of the oboe to represent a bird. Haydn, for example, uses the instrument to represent a hen in the symphony of that name (No. 83, 1785) and the crowing cock in his oratorio *The Seasons* (1801).

BERLIOZ: *SYMPHONIE FANTASTIQUE*

Once again, it is the oboe's lyrical pastoral qualities that are exploited by the composer. Written quickly during the early months of 1830, Berlioz's 'Episode in an Artist's Life' (*Symphonie fantastique* is actually only the work's subtitle) evokes many favourite Romantic themes, including a high-society ballroom, shepherds in the fields and bachanalian devilry. The slow movement, entitled 'Scène aux champs' ('In the meadows') explores the artist's melancholy and uses a cor anglais and an off-stage oboe to represent the piping of the shepherds.

PROKOFIEV: *PETER AND THE WOLF*

Written in 1936, Prokofiev's musical entertainment for children is one of the most often-quoted examples of instruments being used directly to represent characters in a story. In this case some of those characters are animals from the forest (the bird and the wolf, for example) and some are human (including Grandfather, the hunters and, of course, Peter). Prokofiev even represents the sounds of the hunters' guns using timpani. By featuring different instruments for each character, each with its own identifiable theme, the music even educates while it entertains. In the story the duck is represented by an oboe with a rather lugubrious theme (at first in any case), which makes the most of the oboe's lyrical qualities, particularly in its lower register, while remaining tonally close to the distinctive squawk of a duck.

 CLARINET

IN A WORLD OF musical instruments dominated by double reeds, the arrival of the single-reeded *chalumeau* in the late 17th century caused something of a stir. The instrument was far from flexible, having a compass of less than an octave and a half and no capacity to overblow. It did, however, precipitate the invention of the clarinet in the early 1700s.

There is some confusion as to who was responsible for 'inventing' the clarinet, largely due to uncertainty over what actually distinguishes a clarinet from a *chalumeau*. It may be that each was designed to operate in its namesake register (see below), though the instruments were such close cousins at their time of origin that attempts to draw any distinction between them are barely useful. The invention of the clarinet is commonly attributed to one Johann Christoph Denner of Nuremberg, though instruments by his son Jacob were the first to use the name 'clarinet'. It is not even clear if either of the Denners was responsible for the one innovation that could be said to constitute the 'invention' of the clarinet, namely the addition of the 'speaker key' which opens a small hole and allows the instrument to overblow at the 12th (other woodwinds overblow at the octave). The clarinet's early history certainly seems to be cursed by a dearth of reliable information which leaves theories about its birth largely unsubstantiated.

The separate registers that characterized the clarinet during the early years of its development remain a vital part of the instrument's personality today. Constructed in five parts of mouthpiece, barrel, upper joint, lower joint and bell, the modern clarinet's compass is divided into almost as many more or less distinct registers. The *chalumeau* and clarinet registers (the latter has also been labelled *clarion* or *clarino*) constitute the heart of the instrument, with the notorious break or throat register between them, and at the upper end of the compass the extreme or acute register.

✀ Improvements

As the *chalumeau* was gradually superseded by the clarinet, technical improvement became vital. The clarinet did not achieve popular appeal until the last quarter of the 18th century, by which time J. C. Denner's original two-keyed instrument had become decidedly more sophisticated. In England five-keyed clarinets made more primitive models obsolete by 1770, and on the Continent the introduction of larger tone-holes helped to create a more satisfactory *chalumeau* register. Difficulties of fingering meant that the clarinet appeared in several transposing versions, most commonly C and B flat. However, these fully-chromatic instruments still suffered shortcomings in terms of intonation and sound quality, despite attempts around 1785 to provide a more efficient tuning mechanism by separating the mouthpiece and the barrel. The problems persisted until Iwan Müller, one of the most influential German players of his day, developed his thirteen-keyed instrument in about 1812. The new clarinet's tone-holes were positioned with greater acoustical accuracy, achieving much improved intonation, and a new fingering system allowed performance in any key. Indeed, such was Müller's confidence in his clarinet that he grandly claimed it was no longer necessary to use different instruments. The player's enormous influence encouraged the widespread adoption of his clarinet, and it remained very popular until the late years of the 19th century.

ABOVE: UNUSUAL MEMBERS OF THE CLARINET FAMILY: (FROM LEFT TO RIGHT) BASS CLARINET, BASSETT HORN AND ALTO CLARINET.

TYPES OF
Clarinet
❦

OCTAVE CLARINETS in C, B flat and A
Early to mid-19th century. High-pitched
'piccolo' clarinets often employed in military or folk contexts and now obsolete. Italy
was their probable country of origin.

CLARINETTO SESTINO IN A FLAT
c. 1839. A very shrill-toned instrument
designed for military use and often played
with conspicuous virtuosity in Balkan folk-
bands. 'Sestino', diminutive of Italian sesto
('sixth'), refers to its pitch of a sixth higher
than, presumably, the sopranino clarinet in
E flat.

SOPRANINO CLARINET IN G Late 18th
century. An obsolete instrument pitched a
semi-tone below the clarinetto sestino.
Once heard in Viennese Schrammel
Quartets (two violins, bass guitar, clarinet),
but an accordion has replaced the clarinet
since c. 1895.

SOPRANINO CLARINETS in F, E, E flat
and D. 18th century. Now obsolete or very
rare, these instruments had mainly military
use and occasional use in the orchestra for
special effect. The sopranino in D was also
once used as a concerto instrument.

SOPRANO CLARINET IN C Early 18th
century. A standard orchestral instrument
until the end of the 19th century.

SOPRANO CLARINET IN B Late 18th cen-
tury. A rare instrument, virtually unknown
today.

SOPRANO CLARINET IN B FLAT Early
18th century. Today's standard orchestral
clarinet.

SOPRANO CLARINET IN A 18th century.
A standard orchestral clarinet, now yielding
to the B flat instrument (entry immediately
above).

BASSET HORN IN G c.1770. Semi-circular
in shape, later angled. This, or a near relative, may be the instrument now called
'basset clarinet' (see below).

BASSET HORN IN F Late 18th century.
A slightly later development of the above,
its pitch standardized at F. The circular or
angled body enters a box containing three
folds of the tube which then gives into the
metal bell. This produces a fuller sound
than that of the standard clarinets. The
weight of the instrument is supported by
a sling or spike.

BASSET HORN IN D Late 18th century.
A rare local example, mainly in Bohemia.

CLARINETTE D'AMOUR IN D 1772.
Called for by J. C. Bach in his opera
Temistocle but otherwise undocumented.
It has been suggested that he meant the
basset horn in D (immediately above).

CLARINETTE D'AMOUR IN A FLAT
c.1760. Similar to the G instrument below
(next entry), but much rarer.

CLARINETTE D'AMOUR IN G c. 1760.
A straight clarinet with a bent brass crook
at the top, three keys and a pear-shaped
bell to give a soft, velvety tone. Still current
in the Middle East but obsolete in the West.

'BASSET CLARINET' IN G c. 1789.
A mysterious instrument developed by
Anton Stadler with a range extending four
semi-tones below the standard clarinet.
It may equate with the basset horn in G,
though Stadler probably introduced modifications.

CLARINETTE D'AMOUR IN F Early 19th
century. Also called 'tenor clarinet', a
version of the G instrument (entry immediately above).

TODAY'S STANDARD ORCHESTRAL
CLARINET IN B FLAT DATES FROM THE
EARLY 1700s.

Perhaps, inevitably, it was the influence of Theobald Boehm's ground-breaking work with the flute that ultimately dimmed the music world's enthusiasm for Müller's innovations. Boehm himself was not involved in work on the clarinet system that by the 1860s carried his name. Rather, it was the result of a collaboration between the clarinettist Hyacinthe Eleanore Klosé and instrument maker Louis-Auguste Buffet between 1839 and 1843. Buffet was familar with Boehm's work on the flute and, applying some of the same principles, he and Klosé almost completely redesigned the system of tone-holes and keywork. The result was the instrument that is in most use today.

The modern clarinet has a similar, if more refined, quality of sound to that of 1716 when Vivaldi first used it in his oratorio *Juditha triumphans*. Quite different, however, was the piercing tone of the clarinets pitched in D, G and A (as opposed to Vivaldi's in C and D) used by Johann Melchior Molter, a prolific court composer in Karlsruhe, who composed the first six concertos for a solo clarinet around 1745, although one source reports a performance of a clarinet concerto played by a Mr Charles in Dublin three years earlier. It is possible that what Mr Charles played was a concerto for flute or oboe arranged for clarinet.

When Mozart came to London as an eight-year-old in 1764, he was lent a symphony by the German composer Karl Friedrich Abel and was given the exercise of adapting the oboe parts for clarinets. Because the work was now in Mozart's handwriting, it was for nearly two centuries regarded as authentic, given the Köchel number 18 and titled Mozart's Symphony No. 3. Later,

Mozart wrote two major works for clarinet: a Quintet in A, K581 (1789) and a Concerto, K622, both for his friend Anton Stadler. Stadler favoured a now obsolete clarinet in G, a lower-pitched instrument recently dubbed 'basset clarinet', but Mozart's Concerto, originally in G (1789, but re-written by him in A in 1791), was arranged for the standard A clarinet before its first publication in 1801.

℘ Today's Clarinet

The clarinet has appeared in many varieties during its short history. The standard instruments today are in A and B flat. In the 19th century the clarinet was a permanent member of the orchestra as well as an effective concerto and chamber instrument. Weber wrote two concertos for it in 1811, and Louis Spohr contributed four between 1808 and 1828. Brahms's Clarinet Quintet (1891) and Nielsen's Concerto (1928) are among many works to display the standard clarinet's capabilities.

The unusual, stark high-pitched sound of the E flat clarinet has also been used to good effect. Berlioz included one in his *Symphonie fantastique* (1830) as did Richard Strauss in *Till Eulenspiegel* (1895). More recently, Messiaen's *Quartet for the End of Time* (1940) contains an affecting clarinet solo and Stockhausen explored in depth its exotic and virtuosos possibilities in five pieces entitled *Amour* (1974–6). These call for extreme ranges of pitch and dynamic, rasping tone, flutter-tonguing and, in *The Butterflies are Playing*, an amazing effect in which the key 'plops' represent insects' flapping wings. 𝄢

𝄞 THE CLARINET AND SAXOPHONE ARE TWO OF THE MOST POPULAR JAZZ INSTRUMENTS. DUETTING HERE ARE A CLARINET AND (RIGHT), IN THE HANDS OF VIRTUOSO SIDNEY BECHET, A SOPRANO SAX

THE CLARINET IN *Jazz* ℘

When the American bandmaster Patrick Sarsfield Gilmore put together his band in 1878, he established an instrumental line-up that remains typical, including the ubiquitous clarinet. Even before a true jazz idiom emerged, the clarinet featured in cakewalk and ragtime in American minstrel shows of the late 19th and early 20th centuries. Similarly, in the traditional and Dixieland jazz 'combos' of New Orleans, a clarinet could usually be found in the front line alongside cornet and trombone.

In the 1920s the 'blues' of players like Johnny Dodds kept the clarinet in the limelight, but it was during the revolutionary 'swing era' from the mid-1930s to mid-1940s that the jazz clarinet made its mark; never before, or since, was the clarinet so at home in popular music. The swing years were ruled by an undisputed 'King of Swing', clarinettist Benny Goodman. "Goodman is now making jazz history in Chicago," ran one 1936 review. Goodman did more than most to establish the style and popularity of swing jazz. His numbers were often better suited to the concert hall than the ballroom. They featured clarinet playing of show-stopping virtuosity and imagination (his intimate quartet version of the Lockhart/Seitz tune *The World is Waiting for the Sunrise* is a notable example), and some of them, like *Clarinet à la King* and *Scarecrow*, have become timeless jazz anthems.

During the 1940s jazz underwent a stylistic transition from swing to be-bop, later to become 'modern jazz'. With the change, the clarinet lost some prominence in favour of the saxophone in the hands of Coleman Hawkins, Charlie Parker, Stan Getz and others. Today, however, alongside the saxophone, the clarinet still forms an important part of the reed player's armoury.

♭ BASSOON

KNOWN VARIOUSLY AS the 'gentleman' and the 'clown' of the woodwinds, the bassoon is an instrument whose compass and range of tonal colour make it one of the most versatile members of the orchestra. Oddly, even the most exhaustive of studies seems to have failed in pinpointing the origin of the bassoon. This may well be due to the inconsistent and often ambiguous naming of the instrument, though the bassoon's immediate ancestor was almost certainly the *dulcian* or *curtal*. The 17th-century English musicologist James Talbot was among the first, in about 1695, to identify a 'basson in four joynts' and the anglicized version 'bassoon' came into use after it appeared in Purcell's 1691 score *The History of Dioclesian*. However, the one-piece *curtal* seems only to have been finally displaced by the bassoon proper, with its four-joint construction, in the 18th century.

Early bassoons were developed by makers such as the Denners in Nuremberg, who built the first three-key model and later one with four keys which remained standard for most of the 18th century. This instrument also displayed advances in terms of tone colour, becoming more mellow and expressive. It was more capable technically and allowed composers like Telemann in his early Sonata (1728) and Mozart in his Concerto (1774) to write characterful and demanding music. The bassoon had always played an important role as a continuo instrument at the bass of ensemble music (indeed, the original French form of its name, *basson*, indicated simply the bass-register version of any instrument, for example *basson de hautbois* or *basson flûte*). With the rise of the 19th-century solo virtuoso-composer, demands for the bassoon's range to be extended upwards increased, as did the need for louder-toned instruments with more reliable intonation. The problems were not suc-

cessfully tackled until Carl Almenräder (hailed by Curt Sachs as the 'Boehm of the bassoon') developed his fifteen-key instrument around 1820. From 1831 onwards Almenräder collaborated with Johann Adam Heckel in developing the bassoon further. The Heckel family have since continued the work and today produce one of the two versions of bassoon in common use, the other being a French model by the Parisian firm Buffet-Crampon.

✄ *In Performance*

The bassoon's career as a solo and chamber instrument began very early in its life. By the early 1600s the bassoon was beginning to find its feet in an independent role outside the *basso continuo*. The first composition for solo bassoon was a Fantasia by the Venetian Salaverde which appeared around 1638, followed some years later by Bertoli's set of nine sonatas, the first such set for any one instrument. The bassoon was also quickly accepted as an integral part of the developing orchestra and its value as the bass part of wind chamber groups was beginning to figure in composers' thinking.

The arrival of the new jointed bassoon, with its greater possibilities for expressive playing, gave considerable impetus to writing for the instrument. During the 18th and 19th centuries music for the bassoon as a solo and ensemble instrument appeared in abundance. It featured as a key *obbligato* instrument in several of J. S. Bach's cantatas. There were sonatas, concertos and *concertante* symphonies by composers such as Haydn, Paganini and Weber, to name just a few. Chamber music featuring the bassoon was also

♭ THE MODERN ORCHESTRAL BASSOON SECTION, USUALLY CONSISTING OF AT LEAST ONE PAIR OF STANDARD BASSOONS, SITS AT THE BACK OF THE WOODWIND, NEXT TO THE CLARINETS.

on the increase, large numbers of works for bassoon and strings appearing around the turn of the 19th century by Karl Stamitz, Krommer, Danzi and many of their contemporaries. Neither has the bassoon's popularity waned during the 20th century. There are notable solo, *concertante* and chamber works by Elgar, Villa-Lobos, Strauss, Hindemith, Prokofiev and Dutilleux. Even the avant-garde sound world of Stockhausen has exploited the bassoon's versatility in works such as the wind quintet *Adieu* (1966). ⑃

RIGHT: CLEAR SIMI-
LARITIES IN DESIGN
AND USE SUGGEST THE
CURTAL OR *DULCIAN* WAS
THE TRUE FORERUNNER OF
THE BASSOON.

A CLOWN AND A
Gentleman

※

Both the bassoon's comic reputation and its capacity for a more lyrical mode of expression have proved sources of inspiration for composers since the instrument's early days.

VIVALDI: If any composer has managed to combine both characteristics of the bassoon successfully it is Vivaldi, who completed no less than 37 concertos for the instrument. That he wrote so many is curious, for there was no recent tradition of solo bassoon writing in Venice. They were probably composed for the orphanage where he taught, though two (RV502 and 496) appear to be dedicated to local musicians. Along with agile material that skips between the bassoon's bass and tenor registers, Vivaldi includes lyrical passages that belie the instrument's reputation for jocularity.

DUKAS: Of all the works that introduce the bassoon as the clown among instruments, Dukas' famous depiction of a bewitched mop lumbering off to fetch its own bucket of water, in *The Sorcerer's Apprentice* (1897), must be the favourite. As the young, disastrously inexperienced sorcerer casts his spell, Dukas introduces the theme of the work in a phrase that exposes the clowning bassoons at their pompous best.

STRAVINSKY: Further use of the bassoon to comic effect can be found towards the end of Stravinsky's ballet *Pulcinella* (1920). At the other end of the spectrum, though, is his ballet *The Rite of Spring* (1913), depicting a solemn pagan rite associated with the violent eruption of spring in Russia. The ballet opens with an extremely demanding and exposed bassoon solo derived from a Lithuanian folk tune and pitched high in the instrument's top register. Its peculiar and remote sound, about as far as it is possible to be from most people's perception of the 'clowning' bassoon, provides an appropriately mystical opening to this raw and passionate music. Stravinsky used the same effect later in his *Symphonies of Wind Instruments* (1920, revised 1945–7).

BARTOK: The second movement of this composer's Concerto for Orchestra (1943) is another example of the bassoon as 'gentleman' to listen for.

SAXOPHONE

duced the saxophone to their wind bands. It is believed to have made its first appearance in England at a concert promoted by the ill-fated French impresario Louis Jullien in about 1850.

OF ALL THE MEMBERS of the woodwind family, the saxophone is the most modern and probably the most familiar among non-musicians. The instrument's role in popular music idioms, particularly jazz, has afforded it the sort of exposure that is not typical among other woodwinds. It is also the one instrument whose genesis can be quite clearly identified, though the reasons for its taking the shape it did remain rather more of a grey area.

✸ Construction

Antoine Joseph or Adolphe Sax was a Belgian instrument-maker who had long sought a solution to the weak link in contemporary military bands – the lack of an instrument that satisfactorily filled the tonal gap between the clarinets and the tenor brass. Combine this with the suggestion that Sax also dreamed of inventing a clarinet that would overblow at the octave (instead of the 12th), as well as replacing all the woodwinds in a military band with a more powerful group of instruments, and it becomes clear that Sax was an inventive musician with no mean amount of vision. Sax had found what he believed to be the answer by about 1845, though the idea was not an entirely original one. By falling back on the first principles of acoustics he realized that he was looking for a single-reed instrument with a conical bore, rather than the cylindrical bore of the clarinet. A Scot named William Meikle had come to the same conclusion some time earlier and had experimented along these lines with his alto bassoon of 1830. Earlier still, the French instrument-maker Desfontenelles had produced a wooden instrument with a mainly conical bore,

though this was subsequently found to overblow at the 12th.

Sax almost certainly drew inspiration from these crude efforts. He applied the same principles to an instrument that could also carry the new, more sophisticated keywork developed for other woodwinds and produced the first saxophone. By the mid-1840s he had established a successful workshop in Paris and French military bands began using his instruments in preference to clarinets and bassoons. Thanks to the bands' willing adoption of the saxophone, except in Germany, the instrument rapidly found its primary function in popular music. This was particularly so in America where from 1890 onwards John Philip Sousa and his peers intro-

THE TENOR SAXO-PHONE IN B FLAT IS PERHAPS THE MOST EASILY RECOG-NIZABLE MEMBER OF THE FAMILY.

✸ In Performance

Conversely, the instrument was slow to find its way into symphonic music, with at first only French composers like Delibes, Saint-Saëns and Bizet using it. In fact, such was the dearth of specialist saxophonists that Richard Strauss had great difficulty finding four for the premiere of his *Symphonia domestica* in New York in 1904. Happily, the mellow and peculiarly 'vocal' tone of the saxophone has since found a more regular place in the orchestra. Perhaps the best-known example is its role of the troubadour singing at the gate of 'The Old Castle' in Ravel's orchestration (1922) of Mussorgsky's *Pictures at an Exhibition*. Other composers have exploited its sound, including Vaughan Williams in *Job* (1930) and his Sixth Symphony (1947), Prokofiev in *Romeo and Juliet* (1936) and Britten in *Billy Budd* (1951).

At the hands of modern virtuosos like John Harle the saxophone has found its place in the 'art music' of the late 20th century. Harle's popular persona and performances of music by composers such as Dominic Muldowney and Sir Harrison Birtwistle have helped blur the distinction between classical and jazz saxophone. However, it is in the world of jazz that many people believe the saxophone belongs. The saxophone has a noble heritage as a jazz instrument, thanks to gifted exponents like Charlie Parker and, more recently, Courtney Pine and Andy Sheppard. 𝄢

AMERICAN SAXOPHONIST CHARLIE PARKER, PICTURED IN 1949, BECAME SYNONYMOUS WITH THE POST-'SWING' ERA OF MODERN JAZZ.

TYPES OF
Saxophone

※

Sax's patent granted in 1846 covered no fewer than fourteen instruments divided into two groups of seven, one for miltary bands and one for the orchestra. The saxophone family today consists of seven instruments, the most common being soprano, alto, tenor and baritone. Some jazz musicians have extended the top of the range by up to an octave, but the sounding compasses indicated are those found in normal use.

SOPRANINO IN E FLAT

D flat' – A flat'''. Rarely heard but still in production. Ravel used one in his *Boléro*, but that part is now usually taken by a soprano instrument.

SOPRANO IN B FLAT

A flat – E flat''. Made famous by the 1920s jazz player Sidney Bechet, but outside jazz it is only usually heard today in saxophone quartets.

ALTO IN E FLAT

D flat – A flat''. First saxophone to appear in the symphony orchestra, in Thomas's *Hamlet* (1868).

TENOR IN B FLAT

A flat – E flat''. The most popular saxophone in jazz, used in the orchestra later than the alto. An earlier model in C was successful in the United States.

BARITONE IN E FLAT

C – A flat'. A popular jazz instrument; for example, through Gerry Mulligan in the 1950s. Also used by Stockhausen in *Carré* (1960).

BASS IN B FLAT

A flat' – E flat'. Rarely heard outside full saxophone ensembles.

CONTRABASS IN E FLAT

D flat' – A flat. Very rare, only made to order today.

HORN

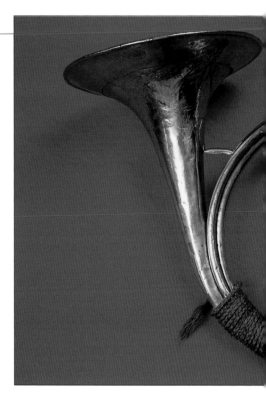

SINCE ANTIQUITY, WHEN simple animal horns were used for sending signals, the horn has been a symbol of power and strength. Whether in Europe, Africa or Asia, horns have served similar purposes, and though individual instruments may have been distinguishable through their sound or appearance, the horn's rural beginnings still find themselves reflected in the instrument's association with things pastoral.

The horn we are concerned with is the European orchestral horn, more commonly called the French horn, due to the supposed origins in France of an instrument close in principle to the one we know today. Of all the winds, the French horn has undergone some of the most interesting technological modifications during its history. From the early simple hoop-like instrument to today's sophisticated 'double' horn, makers have been faced with severe acoustical obstacles in the quest for a fully chromatic instrument that is both reliable and convenient to use. Though it remains one of the most taxing instruments to play well, the mellow tone produced by its small funnel-shaped mouthpiece makes it an enduring favourite. Not only can it stand out in a large modern orchestra, where four or more may be found, but it mixes well with woodwind in the more intimate setting of a wind quintet. It has a fine reputation, too, as an effective soloist in both sonata and concerto.

BELOW: BARRY TUCKWELL HAS INSPIRED WORKS FOR SOLO HORN BY SEVERAL MODERN COMPOSERS, INCLUDING THEA MUSGRAVE'S CONCERTO.

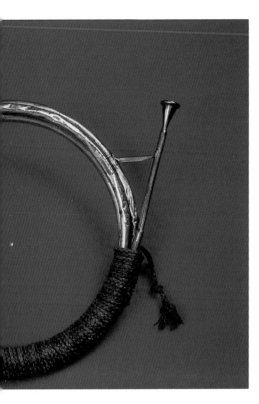

{ FAR LEFT: THE SINGLE-LOOP BUGLE, DEVELOPED IN THE 18TH CENTURY FOR MILITARY USE.

{ LEFT: FOR ALL THE COMPLEXITY OF THE MODERN ORCHESTRAL HORN, ITS 17TH-CENTURY ANCESTOR WAS A SIMPLE TRIPLE-COILED INSTRUMENT.

the name 'French horn' by the early 1600s and this corresponds with the date of the Grand Tour of Count von Sporck from Bohemia who encountered the horn in Paris. The instrument was quite a novelty to him, suggesting that it was unknown outside France. It was not until about 1717 that French horns were heard in an English orchestra, when Handel included them in his *Water Music*. These early horns were constructed in a single piece, so players had to use instruments of different lengths with each key change.

℁ Crooks & Hands

In Vienna Michael Leichnamschneider developed a means of addressing this problem. He introduced a system of 'crooks' (separate rings of

℁ Early Construction

If there is one property that gives the French horn a tone quite distinct from other brass instruments, it is the conical shape of its bore, though the development of playing techniques such as 'hand-stopping' have also helped define this instrument's very individual character. Originally the European horn came from the fields, where hunting and military horns were in widespread use by the late 14th century. Huntsmen and militia remained the horn's principal users almost until the end of the 17th century, although by this time two more advanced horns were in use. Of these the close-coiled *trompe Maricourt* represented an early stage in the development of the hoop-like orchestral horn, the instrument thought to have been used in Lully's comedy ballet *La princesse d'Elide* (1664). From this time on horns became increasingly popular for providing fanfare effects in musical dramas.

Although there is no proof that the horn originated in France there are clear indications that support the theory. The English were using

---

TYPES OF
Horn
℁

HUNTING HORN A high, lively sounding instrument used for important signals during fox or stag hunts. It is known to have existed as early as the 14th century, and later in three versions: English, German and French. The English hunting horn is a short, straight instrument dating from the time of Charles II, while the German circular version was introduced in late 19th century. The French *trompe de chasse* is a large, circular instrument and a direct antecedent of the orchestral horn. Haydn quotes one of the common French hunting horn calls in *The Seasons* (1801). Their typical 6/8 rhythm influenced Mozart in the rondo finales of his horn concertos.

POSTHORN Originally used to signal the arrival and departure of postboys on horseback and later by guards on mail coaches. The Continental version dates from the early 17th century and is typically made in a circle of tightly wound coils. Much imitated in music of early 1700s, it later developed into a semi-orchestral instrument. A valved version is said to have been the origin of the cornet in Paris in the 1820s. The English posthorn is long and straight and pitched in A flat. Koenig's famous *Posthorn Galop* (1844) is based on genuine posthorn calls.

SIGNAL HORN Also known as the bugle, it dates back to the Seven Years' War (1756–63) since when it has had mostly military use in both Europe and America. Originally a large semicircular horn, it was developed into single-loop form around 1700. The present two-loop form was adopted after the Crimean War (1853–6), although the one-loop version is still sometimes preferred on the Continent. It is rarely seen outside military use: Suppé quotes a bugle call at the opening of *Light Cavalry* (1866) and Britten's *Noye's Fludde* (1957) uses an actual bugle.

ORCHESTRAL HORN Operates on the same acoustical principle as other brass instruments, but physical differences determine its distinctive tonal character. The modern horn is an intricately coiled tube nearly 3.5 metres (c. 11 feet) long with a narrow, funnel-shaped mouthpiece. Its conical bore ends with a large bell 28–35cm (c. 11–14 inches) in diameter. The horn was once described as "the most refined and poetical voice in the symphony orchestra", but the technique it requires is the most difficult of all the orchestral instruments to master, which may explain why concertos for it are rare and of short duration.

tubing in different lengths) which allowed the horn to be put into any key required. By now composers like Bach and Handel were writing quite high and florid horn parts, probably the best known Baroque concerto with horns being Bach's First 'Brandenburg' Concerto. Although it was becoming apparent that the clumsiness of instruments with loose crooks was far from ideal, no alternative appeared until the early 19th century.

Meanwhile, makers and players continued to experiment. The Dresden player Anton Joseph Hampl, for example, developed the hand-horn method. This method of performing with the natural horn, first developed by Bohemian players, was refined by Hampl around the mid-1700s. By placing the right hand in the bell and fully or partially stopping the tube, the player could raise or lower notes and fill the gaps in the horn's natural harmonic series. Hampl also invented a new instrument, the *Inventionshorn*, to complement his method of playing (see panel feature) and trained many fellow horn players in its use, including the celebrated Bohemian Giovanni Punto for whom Beethoven composed his Sonata in F, Op.17 (1800).

℅ The Valve Horn

The first moves towards the valve horn we know today came with the development of the 'omnitonic' horn around 1815 (see panel feature). In fact, the first valve horns were patented around the same time but they suffered from deficient valves, particularly in terms of intonation, for at this stage the extra lengths of tubing brought into play by the valves did not include any tuning mechanism. Although the valve horn was not readily accepted in official circles (it did not become the recognized instrument at the Paris Conservatoire until 1903), composers began to include it in their scores. It made its orchestral debut in Jacques Halévy's opera *La juive* (1835), the work that brought the composer fame. Schumann, too, was among the first to write for the valve horn with his Adagio and Allegro in A flat, Op. 70, for horn and piano, and the *Concertstück* in F, Op. 86, for four horns and orchestra, both dating from 1849. The Adagio and Allegro was the first significant solo work for the new valve instrument. The earliest version of the instrument commonly used today, the 'double' horn in F and B flat, first appeared in Germany towards the end of the 19th century.

This was the instrument to benefit from the introduction of a refined piston-valve system patented in 1912, though by the mid-20th century rotary valves had rendered piston valves all but obsolete for the horn.

Against the backdrop of these considerable technical advances, Richard Strauss wrote his demanding Second Horn Concerto in 1942. The circumstances of Strauss's composition of his First Concerto (1882–3) were curiously similar. It came at a time when composers were beginning to write music for the valve horn that extended its range of tonal colour (though interestingly, Brahms persisted in scoring for the hand horn – his Piano Concerto No. 2 in B flat of 1881 opens with a famous passage for hand horns in that same key, B flat). *Glissandos* and 'flutter tonguing' became popular devices, and Debussy made particularly effective use of the horn's adaptable timbre in his *Prélude à l'après-midi d'un faune* (1892–4). However, the concerto

RIGHT: EARLY DEPICTIONS OF THE HORN – THIS ONE DATES FROM THE MIDDLE AGES – CONFIRM ITS BEGINNINGS IN THE HUNTING FIELD.

LEFT: BEFORE THE COMMON APPLICATION OF THE VALVE SYSTEM, HORN PLAYERS USED A SERIES OF DETACHABLE LENGTHS OF TUBING ('CROOKS') TO ALTER THE INSTRUMENT'S KEY.

𝄋

NATURAL HORN Developed from the looped hunting horn of the 15th to 17th centuries. Its first known purely musical use is believed to be an anonymous Czech sonata for strings and *corno da caccia* (1670s). Natural horns in F were known in Germany by 1700 – the earliest example is by the Leichnamschneider brothers of Vienna, dated 1710.

NATURAL HORN WITH CROOKS Invented by the Leichnamschneiders in the early 18th century. The horn was made shorter and a socket incorporated to take additional loops of tubing called 'crooks'. In combination, 'master crooks' and 'couplers' allowed the player to change the instrument's key. This system was superseded after 1750 by a set of up to nine separate crooks, one for each different key.

INVENTIONSHORN Devised by Hampl in about 1750, this allowed crooks to be fitted into the body of the horn (usually onto the inner coil of a two-coil instrument). A similar instrument in France was known as the *cor solo*.

'OMNITONIC' HORN An attempt by Dupont around 1815 to produce a fully chromatic horn without crooks. It included enough built-in tubing to allow the instrument to play in any key and used plungers and sliding shutters, etc., to bring different lengths of tubing into play.

VALVE HORN The earliest example developed by Stölzel and Blühmel in 1818. The most successful were Blühmel's rotary variety, and these are usual today. Modern horns normally have three or four valves – on 'double' instruments in B flat and F, the fourth valve controls about one metre (3 feet) of tubing, modifying a medium-length F horn into a short B flat horn.

had not been seen as an ideal vehicle for the horn due to the strenuous demands of the now highly-developed genre. Indeed, between a minor *concertino* by Weber (1815) and Strauss's First Concerto, very little of consequence was written for solo horn.

The story has been rather different since, with virtuoso players like Aubrey and Dennis Brain, Barry Tuckwell and, recently, Michael Thompson, encouraging leading composers to write for the horn. Both Hindemith and Tippett have written sonatas for four horns; in 1943 Britten composed the Serenade for tenor, horn and strings; and more recently Thea Musgrave and Anthony Powers have written concertos for horn and orchestra (1971 and 1991 respectively).

TRUMPET

AMONG ALL THE INSTRUMENTS of the woodwind and brass families, the trumpet enjoyed the unique, if dubious, distinction of suffering a fall from grace when it joined the orchestra. "Notwithstanding the real loftiness and distinguished nature of its quality of tone," said Berlioz in his *Treatise on Modern Instrumentation and Orchestration* (1843), "there are few instruments that have been more degraded than the trumpet." This 'degradation' concerns the instrument's descent from its highly regarded social function in the 1500s to its often meagre subordinate role in the late-Classical symphony orchestra. In fact, during the trumpet's early history its players were among the first to form a trade union of sorts. From the mid-16th century trumpeters were prized court employees (many Renaissance sovereigns measured their own importance in terms of the number of trumpet ensembles at their disposal). The social distinction between trumpet players and other musicians broadened gradually but noticeably (with kettle drummers, they were often set on raised platforms), and in 1623 an Imperial Guild of Trumpeters was established in the Holy Roman Empire, its function being to control who played the trumpet and where. The trumpeter's protected position served his profession well until around the time of Bach when the trumpet began to be absorbed into the orchestra as a purely *tutti* instrument. From the early 1800s the only relatively secure livelihood for a trumpeter was to be found in the ranks of an orchestra. Notwithstanding the later success of some jazz trumpeters and cornet soloists, it was not until after World War II that the trumpet once again emerged as a solo instrument in orchestral music, in the hands of players like George Eskdale and Helmut Wobisch.

❧ Early History

Just as the horn is distinguished by its conical bore, so the trumpet's bright, perky character is determined to an extent by its cylindrical bore, which has been a constant in the instrument's design since the Middle Ages. The bright sound has always been well suited to military and \ceremonial roles and even in Ancient Egypt trumpets served just this purpose. Two well-known extant examples are the straight silver and bronze instruments rescued from the tomb of Tutankhamun. Curt Sachs claimed that the trumpet disappeared from Europe with the fall of the Roman Empire and did not reappear until around the turn of the second millennium. Even then the trumpeter's social position was far from stable. It was not until the 14th and 15th centuries that players started to find regular employment, typically as tower watchmen, coinciding with early technical development of the instrument itself.

About 1400 the previously straight instrument took on an 'S' shape, shortly afterwards becoming a loop. The use of crooks to change an instrument's key became common, and the slide trumpet was also beginning to appear. Commonly used in church music, this instrument featured telescopic tubing behind the mouthpiece, allowing the player to alter the length of the instrument mid-performance. By the 16th century the trumpet's compass had been extended upwards, and players now began to specialize in performance in specific registers. Of the two main registers, the *principale* (medium) and *clarino* (upper), it was the latter that became the realm of the virtuoso. The label *clarino* proba-

ala gliccaa de muſ
como a fioli dela ſ

EVEN AS EARLY AS THIS 12TH CENTURY ILLUMINATION THE TRUMPET'S IMPORTANCE AS A COURT INSTRUMENT, PARTICULARLY ON CEREMONIAL OCCASIONS, WAS CLEAR.

bly came from 'clarion', the name originally used to distinguish the short ceremonial trumpet from the larger *trumpe* and quoted by Chaucer as early as 1375 in *The House of Fame*. *Clarino* playing was used in Monteverdi's 'musical fable' *Orfeo* (1607), but its most celebrated adoption was by Bach, particularly in the first and third movements of the 'Brandenburg' Concerto No. 2 (c.1721).

TYPES OF
Trumpet

%

TRUMPET IN B FLAT The most common modern instrument used in orchestras, bands and jazz, with a compass of nearly three octaves from e. Its total length of 130cm (over 4 feet) consists of a tapered mouthpipe, holding the mouthpiece, the central section of cylindrical tubing including the tuning-slide, valves and their associated tubing, and a conical bell section ending in a flare about 12cm (5 inches) in diameter. For the valves to give accurate intonation on some notes, particularly in the low register, slides are included to be activated by the player as necessary.

TRUMPET IN D/E FLAT Introduced after the B flat trumpet, probably for performances of music by Bach at the time of his bicentenary in 1885. The Baroque trumpet's principal key was D, but the new model used half the length of tubing. It was pitched in E flat and had alternative tuning slides to lower the pitch to D. The penetrating tone of the D trumpet has been used by some more recent composers including Ravel in *Boléro*, Stravinsky in *The Rite of Spring* and Britten in *Peter Grimes* (1945). These parts are now often played on the piccolo trumpet.

PICCOLO TRUMPET IN B FLAT This was used for the first time around 1906 for a performance of Bach's Brandenburg Concerto No. 2. Pitched an octave above the standard B flat instrument, it has now superseded the trumpet in D/E flat. In principle it is built in the same form as the normal B flat instrument, though it has appeared in a wide variety of shapes. It may also be pitched in A, using alternative slides, and it usually has a fourth valve to allow performance of notes below concert e'.

BASS TRUMPET Specially designed to specifications from Wagner for use in his *Ring* cycle. Wagner originally imagined a huge instrument pitched an octave below the valve trumpet in F with which he was familiar. The actual instrument is only slightly longer than the standard F trumpet, and is pitched in C, sounding an octave below the normal B flat trumpet, with crooks for B flat and A. It has a more mellow tone than other trumpets and has an impressive compass of three octaves from G flat. Some commentators maintain this instrument is more properly a valved trombone than a trumpet; it is certainly usually played by a trombonist.

THIS MID-19TH CENTURY ENGLISH SLIDE TRUMPET IN F BY LONDON MAKERS KÖHLER & SON DEMONSTRATES THAT EVEN AFTER THE INTRODUCTION OF VALVES OTHER EXPERIMENTS CONTINUED.

✄ *Valve Trumpet*

By now new musical styles were emerging which favoured the oboe, flute and violin, so trumpet writing fell into decline. Ironically, at the same time the instrument began to undergo some of its most radical and successful technical develop-

ment. There were several attempts at producing a fully chromatic trumpet, including the 'key trumpet' for which both Haydn and Hummel wrote their popular concertos. More successful was the 'stop trumpet', an instrument made short enough to allow the player to stop the bell with his hand. This principle was first introduced on the trumpet by Michael Wöggel in 1777, some 20 years

after A.J. Hampl used the same technique for the horn (see page 34). A later improvement came with A.F. Krause's *Inventionstrompeten* in the 1790s which incorporated a tuning slide in the body of the instrument. However, as with the horn, it was the successful development of valves, attributed to Stölzel and Blühmel of Berlin, that made truly chromatic trumpets possible. The

CONCERTOS FOR THE
Trumpet

VIVALDI: CONCERTO FOR TWO TRUMPETS IN C, RV537

Vivaldi contributed only this virtuoso work to the trumpet repertoire. Why he did not write more solo material for the instrument is not entirely clear. It may have been that trumpets were not often played by the girls in the orphanage for whom he wrote most of his concertos. Instruments were probably brought in from outside to perform works like the Concerto. Vivaldi certainly recognized the value of the trumpet to the developing orchestra, and when trumpets were not available he used oboes and even violins to simulate them.

GEORG PHILIPP TELEMANN

In 1718 Telemann said about his concertos, "I must own that since the concerto form was never close to my heart it was indifferent to me whether I wrote a great many or not." So it is perhaps surprising to realize that he contributed in excess of 100 fine examples to the genre. These include six for trumpet which, though not too demanding on the whole, allow the player great scope for spirited playing.

HAYDN: CONCERTO IN E FLAT

This was among the works to figure in the trumpet's resurgence as a solo instrument, after a lengthy fallow period lasting from the early 19th century to around 1945. The last of the composer's purely orchestral music, it was written in 1796 after Haydn had returned to Vienna from London to retire. The solo part was written for a rudimentary keyed *clarino* in E flat, designed and played by Anton Weidinger, a trumpeter in the Viennese Court Opera Orchestra. It was for this same instrument that Hummel later wrote his concerto.

HUMMEL CONCERTO IN E FLAT

The Trumpet Concerto in E flat is probably one of the most popular and regularly heard constituents of the trumpeter's repertoire. However, so swamped is it by the volume of the rest of Hummel's output that little is known about the circumstances of this charming work's creation. It probably dates from the end of 1803, shortly before Hummel was appointed as *Konzertmeister* to Prince Nikolaus Esterházy, where Haydn was the (ostensibly retired) *Kapellmeister*.

℅ In Performance

Remarkably little music has been composed for the solo trumpet since Haydn and Hummel. Among the most recent pieces are Poulenc's Triple Sonata for trumpet, horn and trombone (1922) and Hindemith's Sonata (1939). During the 20th century it is in the jazz world that the trumpet has made its mark, thanks largely to Louis Armstrong, whose importance is difficult to overstate. Armstrong set the standard for jazz trumpet playing in many ways: he was the first trumpeter, for example, to extend the instrument's range up to f''' (concert pitch $e\,flat'''$). He actually started out playing the cornet and only came to the trumpet later. His contemporary Bix Beiderbecke followed the same route, and Beiderbecke's so-called 'Chicago style' of lyrical improvisation became a model still taken up by jazz trumpeters today. Other important players have included Dizzy Gillespie in the 'be-bop' era and Miles Davis who played 'cool jazz'. Between them, these two demonstrated the enormous tonal range of the trumpet. Gillespie was an extrovert showman known for his nonchalant bravado and breathtaking virtuosity. By contrast, Davis played very few notes to Gillespie's many per second but their *vibrato*-less emotion and colour were unequalled. The current generation of jazz trumpeters includes Winton Marsalis who, in 1993, became the first jazz trumpeter to perform with his own ensemble at the BBC Henry Wood Promenade Concerts in London. ⑬

'stop trumpet' continued to be used until well into the 19th century, but it was for the valve instrument that Berlioz and Rossini wrote parts in *Les francs-juges* (1826) and *William Tell* (1829) respectively. Towards the end of the 19th century trumpet parts in music by Wagner, Mahler and Richard Strauss made such demands on the typical F trumpet that players began to change to shorter, and therefore higher, instruments in B flat and C. It is the B flat valve trumpet that has endured to become the most commonly used today.

𝄞 RIGHT: THE B FLAT TRUMPET IS THE STANDARD INSTRUMENT IN USE TODAY.

𝄞 LEFT: WINTON MARSALIS REPRESENTS FOR MANY THE BENCHMARK AGAINST WHICH MODERN JAZZ PLAYING SHOULD BE MEASURED.

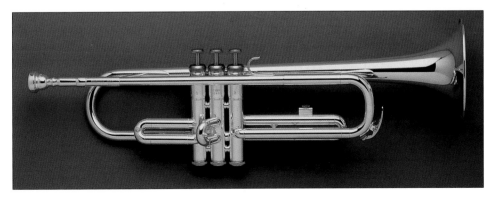

TROMBONE

ONCE DESCRIBED BY the sharp-witted conductor Sir Thomas Beecham as a "quaint and antique drainage system", the trombone occupies a special place in the woodwind and brass families. It is unique in being the one naturally chromatic wind instrument. This is due to the slide which corresponds to the valves used by other brass instruments, but which antedates valves by some four centuries.

The trombone, or 'sackbut' as the English then preferred to call it, originated in the 15th century, apparently as a modified version of the slide trumpet. The principles of design established for the instrument then have largely held good until the present day. The most noticeable physical difference between the early instrument and its successors was the almost complete lack of a flaring bell, which did not appear until around 1740 when players and composers began to demand a stronger sound.

⅍ In Performance

The trombone was used extensively for royal ceremonies and feasts, often paired with the cornett, a small, curved, wooden horn. The same combination of trombones and cornetts was also common in churches. The trombone began to find a place in ensembles accompanying opera, a notable example being Monteverdi's *Orfeo* (1607). Both Giovanni Gabrieli and Heinrich Schütz made good use of the instrument as did Matthew Locke in *Music for His Majesty's Sagbutts and Cornetts* (1661). The trombone was not adopted as an orchestral instrument until the late-18th century. The wind music fashions of that century were led by the French, who avoided

using the trombone after Lully abolished it from court ensembles in the 1660s. Consequently, little of significance was written for the trombone for much of the 18th century.

With the adoption of the trombone into military bands and as a bass strengthener in the orchestra around the turn of the 19th century, the instrument could at last be said to have come of age. It was probably inevitable that the experimentation with valves on brass instruments around 1820 would include the trombone. Happily, their limited success meant a quick return to the slide, and the instrument was none the worse for diversion. By the Romantic period of the mid- to late-18th century the trombone had developed a reputation as a highly expressive instrument, yet the development around 1850 of trombones with wider bores seemed only to encourage composers to use the instrument as much for its loudness as its capacity for subtler emotional colouring. It is the brazen side of the trombone's character with which audiences remain most familiar, for little has been done during the 20th century to redress the balance. Having inspired only a handful of solo works,

THE DISTINCTIVE SHAPE OF THE TROMBONE HAS NOT CHANGED MUCH SINCE THE INSTRUMENT'S INCEPTION. COMPARE THE MODERN ORCHESTRAL TYPE (ABOVE) WITH THE SACKBUT (RIGHT).

including a delightful concerto (1952) by Gordon Jacob and Sandström's remarkable *Motorbike* Concerto of 1969, the trombone remains a relative stranger to the solo platform.

In common with other instruments of the Renaissance and Baroque periods the trombone was produced in several sizes in its early days. Michael Praetorius identified four varieties of trombone: alto, tenor, bass and contrabass. In addition the recent trombone family has included soprano and tenor-bass models. It is the tenor instrument in B flat that finds most common use today. The seven positions of the slide, each lowering the fundamental note by one semitone, and the associated harmonic series give the instrument a compass of about two and a half octaves from *E*. Pitched in B flat an octave above the tenor, the soprano probably appeared in the late 17th century and was called for in scores by Purcell and Bach. Alto trombones, commonly in E flat or F, were used extensively from the 16th to 18th centuries but were often replaced by the tenor thereafter so use of them declined. More recent scores to use the alto trombone include Berg's *Three Orchestral Pieces* (1914) and Britten's church parable *The Burning Fiery Furnace* (1966). The contrabass trombone in B flat or C, an octave below the tenor, has appeared in many variations, usually with a 'double slide', affording extra length without the need for slide positions beyond that of a tenor instrument. The tenor-bass trombone in B flat/F and bass trombone in F are in fairly common use today. Both use one or, in the case of the bass, two valves to bring extra lengths of tubing into play without requiring the player to stretch an unreasonable distance with the slide.

THE TROMBONE'S USE IN THE
Orchestra

℅

BEETHOVEN The first important use of the trombone in a symphony was by Beethoven in his Fifth Symphony (1804-8), which uses normal Classical forces until the finale. After the hushed transition from the C minor third movement to the finale, the trombones make an impressive first appearance as the daylight of C major bursts forward.

SCHUBERT AND WAGNER By the end of the 19th century the trombone was part of the standard resources of an orchestra. It had regained what Berlioz described as its 'epic' character. In 1825 Schubert had used three trombones throughout his 'Great' C major symphony and Wagner composed one of the best known orchestral trombone themes in his *Tannhäuser* overture of 1845.

STRAVINSKY The most famous property of the trombone is its capacity to produce comic *glissandos*. Stravinsky used this to great effect, though more in the style of grotesque parody than comedy. Good examples can be found in his ballets *The Firebird* and *Pulcinella*, both dating from around 1919.

TUBA

ALTHOUGH THE NAME 'tuba' was originally coined by the Romans for their forerunner of the trumpet, the word is now universally associated with that large, fun-loving brass instrument that rumbles away beside the trombones in an orchestra. In fact, the tuba is a remarkably versatile and agile instrument, as solo works by Vaughan Williams, Gordon Jacob, Edward Gregson and Derek Bourgeois demonstrate.

♯ Bass Tuba

The modern tuba has a wide conical bore and between three and six valves, depending on the instrument's size. The tuba family includes some instruments usually known by other names, such as the euphonium and sousaphone – these and other unusual brass instruments are discussed separately (see pages 44–5). Like the saxophone in the woodwinds, the tuba is a relatively recent addition to the brass section, though of course the principles of its design had been established and developed for the trumpet for some considerable time. It was the arrival of Stölzel and Blühmel's piston valve around the 1820s that first prompted the production of brass instruments to operate in the bass register. Wilhelm Wieprecht, bandmaster of Prussian Dragoon Guards and a trombonist by training, produced a 'bass tuba' in collaboration with the Berlin instrument-maker Johann Gottfried Monitz in 1835. The 'bass tuba' may have grown from the seed of the 'Berlin piston valve' also developed by the two men. It was a short valve of unusually large diameter which seemed to Wieprecht and Moritz most suitable for use on a brass instrument with a wide bore. In true chicken and egg style, however, it has already been suggested that the genesis of the 'Berlin valve' actually lay in work already done on the wide-bored 'bass tuba', rather than the other way round.

Whatever the truth of the matter, the first 'bass tubas' laid important groundwork for the instrument familiar today. There were differences in physical appearance, but many of the technical

♯ THE BASS TUBA SUPPLIES THE FOUNDATION OF THE BRASS IN THE MODERN SYMPHONY ORCHESTRA.

characteristics, including being pitched in F, were the same as they are now. Soon after 1835 other makers began to adapt the original 'bass tuba' design to their own purposes, producing tubas in a wide variety of shapes and sizes, some using rotary valves in preference to the Wieprecht/ Monitz *Berliner-Pumpen*.

♯ Wagner Tuba

Berlioz became the first major composer to use the tuba in his works, shortly followed by Wagner who included it in his orchestration for *Der fliegende Holländer*, first performed in 1843. About ten years later, while writing *Das Rheingold*, part one of the *Ring* cycle, Wagner came across the saxhorns being produced by Adolphe Sax in Paris, and he determined to include similar bass instruments in his works

Tuba Concerto

※

In describing the music of his Tuba Concerto, Vaughan Williams said it is "fairly simple and obvious and can probably be listened to without much previous explanation". When it was first performed it was probably the light-hearted image of the tuba, rather than the music, that resulted in the piece not being taken terribly seriously. Instead, it was regarded as something of a romp. This attitude fails to do justice to the work's achievement, particularly in the central Romanza movement, where the composer's efforts to discover all the instrument's capabilities come to light in some beautifully lyrical writing. If the work does have a lighter side, it is in the Finale which has been likened in spirit to an instrumental version of *Falstaff* and the fairies of Shakespearean fame. The Tuba Concerto was premiered in June 1954 by Philip Catelinet and the London Symphony Orchestra (to whom it is dedicated) under the direction of Sir John Barbirolli.

RALPH VAUGHAN WILLIAMS (LEFT) PICTURED WITH SIR JOHN BARBIROLLI WHO CONDUCTED THE FIRST PERFORMANCE OF THE COMPOSER'S TUBA CONCERTO.

horns). Wagner's instrument was later also used by Bruckner in his last three symphonies, Nos 7, 8 and 9, by Richard Strauss and by Schoenberg in *Gurrelieder* (1900–3).

※ The Tuba Range

To this day the proliferation of different sized tubas has persisted, with instruments used in Britain, on the Continent and in America all differing in key. In Britain the E flat tuba is now most common, though in the late 19th century F instruments were typical. American orchestras, meanwhile, used contrabass B flat or E flat instruments. Later, tubas in low C were adopted to replace those in E flat and the F tuba came to be used as necessary to play parts at the upper end of the range. Different again were the French players who typically used 'tenor' tubas in C, and it was probably this instrument that Ravel had in mind when he used a high, muted tuba in *Bydlo*, part of his 1922 orchestration of Mussorgsky's *Pictures at an Exhibition*. Since 1945, the tuba has undergone something of a renaissance, with jazz and avant-garde musicians demonstrating that there is considerably more to this instrument than the 'Tubby' persona typically associated with it. 𝄡

(saxhorns actually ranged in size from sopranino to contrabass). The result of this encounter is the so-called 'Wagner tuba', a hybrid of tuba and French horn with a distinctive oval shape and a wide bore that tapers rapidly towards the mouthpipe so that a horn mouthpiece can be used. Also in common with the horn, it uses rotary valves positioned under the fingers of the left hand rather than the right as in a normal tuba. The similarities mean that in performances of Wagner's *Ring* cycle, four of the eight horn players can double on Wagner tubas, two of them playing tenor instruments in B flat and two bass models in F (the same keys as standard orchestral

A SUB-CONTRA BASS TUBA WITH 34 FEET (10.5 METRES) WHICH CAME TO LIGHT IN 1957 IN THE BASEMENT SHOP OF SOHO (LONDON) INSTRUMENT MAKERS, PAXMAN BROTHERS.

♪ RARE BRASS

(1749). There are also reports of a player in the Prince Regent's private band commissioning an arrangement for serpent of a violin concerto by Corelli. What the instrument lacked in accuracy of intonation it must have made up for in agility!

Although the instruments discussed here are being treated as distinct from the other members of the brass family, and by rights they are, several of them are closely associated with the standard brass through the tuba. Indeed, the euphonium and sousaphone are usually included as members of the modern tuba family.

✕ *Serpent*

Of these 'rare brass' the serpent is the most singular in appearance, with its characteristic undulating shape. However, it is unclear whether it should properly be treated as a brass instrument at all; really, it lies squarely in the no-man's land of plain 'wind'. The serpent's deep sound is half-way between a tuba and a bassoon. It is played like a brass instrument, with a cup-shaped mouthpiece, but its body is wooden and has keyed fingerholes. The instrument is said to have originated in France in the late 1500s to accompany plainchant in church. Towards the end of its life, in the late 19th century, it was used in military bands to support the bassoons' bass part.

The serpent rarely appeared outside church music and military bands, but Handel did include one in his celebratory *Music for the Royal Fireworks*

✕ *Ophicleide*

The ophicleide forms a useful link between the serpent and the euphonium. It is pitched in B flat, the same key as the euphonium, and it shares the same mouthpiece, but in appearance it is closer to an upright serpent (sometimes called 'Russian bassoon'), and it uses keys rather than valves. Though the ophicleide is now obsolete, it was used extensively during the 19th century to provide a bass part in brass and military bands as well as in the orchestra's brass section. When

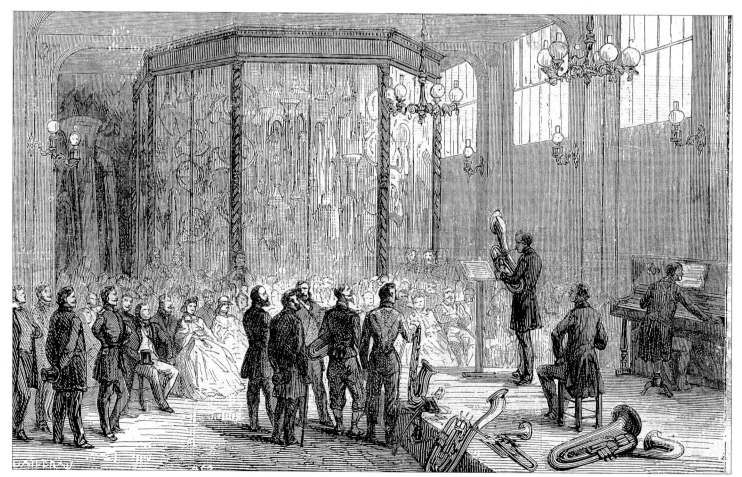

played at its loudest the tone can be powerfully coarse, but the instrument is equally capable of a subtler 'vocal' quality of tone. The adaptable sound made the ophicleide a popular addition to the orchestrator's palette.

✸ Saxhorn

Not satisfied with these other instruments, or with sticking to the saxophone for that matter, the ever-inventive Parisian Adolphe Sax produced, in 1845, the saxhorns. (Incidentally, we might conjecture that this over-expanded his business, for by 1852 Sax was bankrupt.) The saxhorns are closer still to the tubas, with bells pointing upwards (except in the smallest sizes) and *Berliner-pumpen* valves, patented in Germany for the first tubas. In actual fact, instrument-makers across Europe were all developing new brass instruments in different sizes, but Sax was the first to produce a complete family. It is believed to be the larger saxhorns that first prompted Wagner to come up with his own special tubas for the *Ring* (see page 43). The complete saxhorn family comprised nine sizes, from sopranino in B flat (the pitch of the present piccolo trumpet) to a 'sub-bass' model in E flat. The E flat alto remains in use as the tenor horn and the B flat bass is now the euphonium.

Berlioz is probably the best-known user of the saxhorn, having used two in his epic opera *Les Troyens* (1858), one sopranino in B flat and in 'The Royal Hunt and Storm' an E flat alto, though he later rescored the latter part for horn. The tenor horn is closely related to the *flügelhorn* (see below), and the name *flügelhorn* is sometimes mistakenly applied to the sopranino and soprano saxhorns.

✸ Euphonium

It is with the euphonium that we come closest to the modern tuba family. The instrument is usually referred to as the tenor tuba when it is used as an orchestral instrument. Its immediate predecessor is accepted as the bass saxhorn, although its name seems to have been adopted from an 1840s German design, suggesting the influence of the earlier *bombardon* bass tuba from that country. Pitched in B flat, the euphonium has a compass of about three octaves and is most commonly encountered in British brass bands where its velvety tone has an important solo role.

The euphonium has always had a special place as a solo instrument in British brass bands, so players of it are often capable of considerable virtuosity. Many of the 20th century's most important British composers have exploited this, using the euphonium to great effect in their music. They include Elgar, Vaughan Williams, Walton, Tippett and particularly Holst in *The Planets* (1916). Other notable users of the instrument have included Richard Strauss in *Don Quixote* (1897) and Stravinsky in *The Rite of Spring* (1913).

✸ Sousaphone

John Philip Sousa's bass tuba or sousaphone, designed for use in marching bands, was developed from the helicon introduced in Vienna in 1849. The helicon's name came from its 'helical' or spiral design which had tubing encircling the player's body with the instrument's weight carried on his left shoulder. Sousa's very similar version was topped by an enormous bell pointing straight up (a design irreverently dubbed 'the rain catcher'), though after modifications in 1908 it pointed forward to give the now-distinctive shape. This large bell actually serves no special purpose; rather its role is simply to pro-

vide a spectacle at the rear of the band. The sousaphone has also occasionally found its way into jazz ensembles.

✸ Flügelhorn and Mellophone

Of the multitude of other ancient and modern brass rarities, two are particularly worth mentioning. The first is the *flügelhorn*, a cornet-like instrument found in British brass bands and used by British composer Ralph Vaughan Williams in his Ninth Symphony (1956–8). The second is the mellophone, or tenor cor, which, although now very rare indeed, has found use as a jazz instrument and, on occasion, as a replacement for the French horn. 🎼

INDEX
WOODWIND & BRASS INSTRUMENTS

A

Abel, Karl Friedrich 27
Agricola, Martin 18
Almenräder, Carl 28
Armstrong, Louis 39
aulos 11, 20

B

Bach, J.S. 19, 21, 23, 25, 28, 34,
    37, 40
bagpipes 13
Bartók, Béla 29
Basset clarinet 25
Basset horn *24*, 25
bassoon *28*, 28–9
Bechet, Sidney *26*
Beecham, Sir Thomas 40
Beethoven, Ludwig van 17, 19,
    23, 34, 41
Beiderbecke, Bix 39
bells 11, 12
Berg, A. 40
Berio, Luciano 19, 23
Berlioz, L. H. 23, 27, 36, 39, 42,
    45
Bertoli, G. A. 28
Birtwistle, Sir Harrison 30
Bizet, G. 30
Blühmel, F. 35, 38, 42
Boehm, Theobald 17, *18*, 18, 20,
    22, 27
Bohemians 34
Boulez, Pierre 19
bowharp 8, 11
Brahms, J. 27, 34
Brain, Aubrey 35
Brain, Dennis 35
Britten, Benjamin 23, 30, 33, 35,
    37, 40
bugle *32*, 33
bull-roarer 9, 11

C

Cage, John 19
calamellus 20
chalumeau 24
clappers 11
clarinet *24*, 24–7, *25*, *26*
conch shell trumpet *6*, 7
cor anglais (French horn) 21
Corelli, A. 44
curtal 28, *29*

D

Davis, Miles 39
Debussy, C. 19, 21, 34
Delibes, L. 30
Delius, F. 21
Denner, J.C. 19, 24, 28
Desfontenelles 30
drums 10, 11, 12
Dukas, P. 29
dulcian 28, *29*
Dvorák, A. 21

E

Elgar, Sir Edward 29, 45
Eskdale, George 36
euphonium 45

F

flügelhorn 45
flute 10, 11, *17*, 17–19
French horn 33

G

Galway, James 19
Gillespie, 'Dizzy' 39
Gilmore, Patrick Sarsfield 27
Goliards, The 14, 15
Goodman, Benny 27
gourd flute 11
gourd rattle *9*, 9

Gregson, Edward 42

H

Hampl, A J. 34, 38
Handel, G. F. 19, 23, 33, 34, 44
harp 7, 10, 11, 13
Haydn, F.J. 23, 28, 33, 38, 39
Heckel, Johann Adam 28
Hindemith, P. 29, 35, 39
hoboy 20
Holst, G. 45
Horn 11, 12, 13, *32–3*, 32–5, *34*,
    35
Hotteterre, Jean 18, 20
Hotteterre, Jacques *17*
Hummel, J.N. *3*, 39
hunting horn 33
hurdy-gurdy 14
hydraulis *12*

I

Ibert, Jacques 19
inventionshorn 34, 35

J

jazz 27, 39
Jew's harp 9

K

Köhler & Son 37
Krommer, Franz 29

L

Leichnamschneider, Michael
    33–4, 35
Locke, Matthew 40
Lully, J.B. 19, 22, 33, 40
lur *13*
lute 10, *11*, 11
lyre 9, *10*, 10, 11, 12, 13

M

Mahillon, Charles 21
Mahler, Gustav 39
maracas 11
Marsalis, Wynton *38*, 39
Martinu, Bohuslav 23
masroquita 13
Mastersingers, The 14, 15
mellophone 45
Messiaen, Oliver 27
Minnesingers, The *14*, 14, 15
Molter, Johann M. 27
Monitz, Johann Gottfried 42
Monteverdi, C. 40
mouth bow 11
Moyse, Marcel 19
Mozart, W.A. 19, 23, 27, 28, 33
Muldowney, Dominic 30
Müller, Iwan 24, 27
Musgrave, Thea 32, 35

N

Nielsen, Carl 27

O

oboe 9, *20*, 20–23, *22*
omnitonic horn 34, 35
ophicleide 44–5
orchestra 12–13, 23
organ 7, *12*, 12

P

Paganini, N. 28
panpipes 11
Parker, Charlie 27, 30, *31*
piano, thumb 11
piccolo 17
Pine, Courtney 30
pipes 13
posthorn 12, 33
Poulenc, Francis 39

Praetorius, Michael 40
Prokofiev, S. 23, 29, 30
psantrîn 13
Punto, Giovanni 34
Purcell, Henry *22*, 22, 28, 40

Q

qatros 13
Quantz, Johann J. 17, 19
quarna 13

R

rattles *9*, 9, 11
Ravel, M. 17, 19, 30, 37, 43
recorder 9, 11
Rossini, G. 39
Russian bassoon 44

S

sabka 13
Sachs, Curt 12, 17, 28, 36
sackbut 40, *41*
Saint-Saëns, Camille 30
Sax, Adolphe 30, 42, *44*, 45

saxhorn 42–3, 45
saxophone 26, *30*, 30–31
Schubert, F.P. 19, 41
Schumann, R.A. 34
Schütz, Heinrich 40
scraper 9, 11
serpent 44
shawm 20, *22*, 22
Sheppard, Andy 30
Sibelius 21
sistrum 11
Sousa, John Philip 30, 45
sousaphone *45*, 45
Spohr, Louis 27
Stadler, Anton 25, 27
stamping tube 11
Stockhausen, Karlheinz 27, 29
Strauss, Richard 21, 29, 39, 43,
    45
    Concertos 23, 34, 35
    Symphonies 27, 30
Stravinsky, Igor 17, 29, 37, 41, 45
Sumerians, The 11
sumphoniah 13

T

Talbot, James 28
Telemann, G.P. 23, 28, 39
Tippett, Sir Michael 35, 45
trigon 13
trombone *40*, 40–41
trompe de chasse 33
troubadors 14, *15*, 15
Trouvéres 14, 15
trumpet 11, 12, *13*, *36–7*, *37*,
    36–9, *39*
    conch shell *6*, 7
tuba *42*, 42–3, *43*
Tuckwell, Barry *32*, 35
Tutankhamun 11, 36

U

valve horn 34–5
valve trumpet 38–9
Vaughan Williams, Ralph 23, 30,
    42, 42, 45
viol 9
Vivaldi, A. 19, 23, 27, 29, 39

W

Wagner, Richard 15, 37, 39, 41,
    42, 45
Wagner tuba 42–3
Walton, Sir William 45
war trumpet *13*
water organ *12*
Weber, C M von 27, 28, 35
whistle 11, 12
wind ensemble *16*
Wobisch, Helmut 36

X

xylophone 11

Z

zither 11
zmara 13

Woodwind and Brass

The publishers would like to thank the following sources for their kind permission to reproduce the pictures in this book:

AKG London, Bonani, The Bridgeman Art Library, Jean-Loup Charmet, Christies Images, Corbis/Hulton Getty, Mary Evans Picture Library, Maureen Gavin Picture Library, Michael Holford, Hulton Getty, Lebrecht Collection/Maeder, Performing Arts Library/Clive Barda, J McCormick, Pictorial Press, University of Edinburgh/Collection of Historic Musical Instruments, Courtesy Yamaha

Every effort has been made to acknowledge correctly and contact the source and/or copyright holder of each picture, and Carlton Books Limited apologises for any unintentional errors or omissions which will be corrected in future editions of this book.

About the Author

Robert Dearling is a respected classical music writer and reviewer. In addition to being a specialist in the music of the 18th century, he has considerable knowledge of musical instruments and over the past 30 years has amassed a huge database of information pertaining to the histories and uses of the world's instruments. He has a wide knowledge of music journalism and has written for many periodicals. He has also written over 400 sleeve and CD booklet notes for among others, Decca, EMI, RCA and Sony. His books include *The Guinness Book of Music*, *The Guinness Book of Recorded Sound*, and *Mozart – The Symphonies*.